Canada and
the U.S.A.

*A Background Book
about Internal Conflict and
the New Nationalism*

Canada and the U.S.A.

A Background Book about Internal Conflict and the New Nationalism

by Richard J. Walton

Parents' Magazine Press • *New York*

Each Background Book is concerned with the broad spectrum of people, places, and events affecting the national and international scene. Written simply and clearly, the books in the series will engage the minds and interests of people living in a world of great change.

To Richard and Catherine,
who also enjoy their visits to Canada

Contents

Other Books by Richard J. Walton

America and the Cold War

Beyond Diplomacy: A Background Book on American
Military Intervention

Cold War and Counterrevolution: The Foreign Policy of
John F. Kennedy

The Remnants of Power: The Tragic Last Years of
Adlai Stevenson

The United States and Latin America

Author's Note

ALTHOUGH THE WORDS "America" and "American" apply, of course, to the whole western hemisphere and not just to the United States, I have for the sake of editorial convenience used both words as they are commonly, perhaps chauvinistically, used in the United States as referring solely to this country. In referring to our northern neighbor I have used the term British North America (B.N.A.), in the earlier sections, and Canada. I hope that in the context of this book this usage is clear—and forgivable.

There is another problem in connection with "Canada." In the earliest days, Canada meant solely that part of present-day Canada that coincides roughly with the present-day province of Quebec. Later the term was extended to cover what is now, roughly, the province of Ontario. Sometimes the singular, Canada, was used to cover both areas and other times they were referred to as the "two Canadas." At various times what is now Quebec was called "Lower Canada" and "Canada East" and what is now Ontario was termed "Upper Canada" and "Canada West." Until confederation, the other provinces — Nova Scotia, Prince Edward Island, etc. — were considered separate colonies.

A final note about the name Canada itself. No one knows for sure where the name came from, but the best conclusion seems to be that it is derived from the word *Cannata*, believed to be the name for the Indian village at the site of what became Quebec.

—R.J.W.

Foreword

ALTHOUGH THERE ARE many things on which they cannot agree, most Canadians would agree on one thing: that Americans take them for granted. Those of us south of what has been the longest undefended border in the world (a cliché few Americans resist when discussing United States-Canadian relations) do take Canada for granted. We tend to think of it, on those rare occasions when we do think of it, as a nice country, sort of like us, but more placid, and content to follow our lead. A good neighbor, friendly but perhaps a little dull. That may once have been true, but no longer. Things have changed in Canada as they have all over the world. Canadians are tired of being taken for granted and they're no longer willing to play the role of awe-struck kid brother. Seeing all our problems, they no longer are convinced that ours is the model to follow. A new nationalism has arisen in Canada that is often close to anti-Americanism and that may come even closer. Canadians have come to recognize what they have known all along, even if unconsciously: that the United States by its sheer power may, even if it doesn't mean to, absorb Canada economically and culturally if not politically. Many Canadians, among them a high proportion of the brightest, best educated, and most articulate, want to erect defenses along that undefended border. Not military defenses but economic and cultural defenses.

This new nationalism, perhaps not coincidentally, has arisen at a time of crisis, when there is a genuine and well-founded fear that the Canadian union may disintegrate, not only because of the now well-publicized tensions between French-speaking Quebec and the English-speaking rest of the country but also because of the continuing and serious disputes between the federal and the provincial governments. The controversies over this new nationalism aimed at the United States and over the alarming lack of unity caused by the French-English/federal-provincial conflicts have become inextricably interwoven, as they were often in the past.

Americans can no longer ignore this situation, for we are involved, like it or not. Canada is not only a neighbor with much common history and many common traditions, but it is our most important trading partner, more important than all of Western Europe or all of Latin America. Furthermore, Canada is a rich repository of natural resources vital to our economy now and certain to be even more so in the future. How much access we will have to those resources — minerals, petroleum, natural gas, wood, and, perhaps most important of all, water — will determine the shape of our economy, even our standard of living.

There is more to it than economics. The Canadians have long been good friends, allies in three wars, and all but a few Canadians want to be our friends still. But increasingly they insist on their identity as Canadians. They don't want Canada to become a paler United States. They don't want Canada to become an economic colony of the United States. There are those Canadians who say it is already too late to reverse the trend toward continentalism, but growing numbers argue that it is not too late. They are calling out for our attention, even our sympathy, but many are afraid that we are too preoccupied with our own problems to listen. We should listen, however, for our own sakes as well as theirs.

1

The Early Years

TWO STRAINS RUN through Canadian history: a concern over, amounting sometimes to a fear of, American intentions; and the struggle to forge and maintain the unity of a country even vaster than the United States. The first is the older. As Canadian historian Gerald M. Craig has written: "Enmity, antagonism, and competition long precede the emergence of the United States or of Canada as a national entity. . . ." [1]

Indeed, in the beginning there was no United States, no Canada, just North America over which Britain and

France struggled for more than two centuries, a struggle that was to influence the history not only of this continent but of the world. Although centuries later the United States became paramount, it was Canada that first impressed itself, however briefly, on European consciousness. It seems fairly certain that the Norsemen first discovered the New World about the year 1000, making their landfall on what is now Newfoundland. But their colonies did not last long, probably succumbing to the long bitter winters. The memory of that first discovery eventually faded, to be recalled centuries later by scholars. Thus, when John Cabot, sailing for Henry VII of England, also encountered Newfoundland, it was hailed as a great new discovery, and became the basis for the English claim to North America. (This occurred only five years after Columbus, far to the south, had made his discovery.) The French based their claim to North America on the voyages of Jacques Cartier nearly forty years later. Indeed, Cartier's voyages were, in a sense, more important, for on his second expedition he sailed into the St. Lawrence River, which became the highway for the French-American empire.

These early voyages by Cabot, Cartier, and others did not lead to immediate colonization. While the Spanish began to establish colonies almost immediately after Columbus's discoveries, the English and French waited almost a century, no doubt because gold, the great lure for Europeans, had not been discovered, and because of the harsh winters. But the area was not wholly ignored. Fishermen had come upon the inexhaustible supplies of cod off the Grand Banks, possibly even before Cabot's voyage. And the Portuguese had established a commercial fishery early in the sixteenth century. Shortly afterward, Basque fishermen had set up a station at Tadoussac, where the Saguenay River enters the St. Lawrence, to fish, hunt whales, and trade for furs with the Indians.

The French, eventually recognizing the commercial possibilities, created the first permanent European settlement at Port Royal on the Annapolis Basin in Acadia (Nova Scotia) in 1605. From then on, the choice of settlements by the British and French determined the course of North American history. The French decided to penetrate inland, using the St. Lawrence as their highway. Samuel Champlain founded Quebec in 1608. Trois Rivières was founded in 1634, and Montreal in 1642.

During the same decades the British began to establish their colonies in North America, choosing to do so along the Atlantic Coast from Nova Scotia (which swung back and forth between British and French rule) all the way down to Georgia, including Jamestown in 1607, Plymouth in 1620, etc. The first English settlement in what was to become Canada was in Newfoundland in 1610. Yet Newfoundland, the oldest part of English Canada, remained a direct colony of Britain until 1949, waiting almost a century to join the Dominion of Canada, which was established in 1867.

Fully as important as the location of the French and English colonies was their character. Life in New France was nearly as feudal as life at home. The settlers were dominated by the officials sent from France to govern, and the local gentry and clergy had the same conservative influence in America that they had in France. This conservatism, this closeness to the land and the Church, persisted for more than three centuries. Only within the last decade or so have the French-Canadians begun to shake off their ancient traditions. Just as the French were set on their course in the early years, so too were the English. Coming from a land with a parliamentary tradition, the English settlers from the beginning were given a good measure of self-government and, as time went on, they demanded even more. The English, and the Irish and the Scottish, also came from a tradition favorable to trade and commerce, whereas the French often thought of trade as being somewhat less respectable than the professions, or the clergy, or working the land. This, too, as we shall see, had a lasting influence on the history of Canada.

Almost immediately conflict began to break out between French and English settlers, an inevitable consequence of the interminable French and English wars in Europe. As early as 1629 British privateers raided and temporarily held Quebec. That same year Sir William Alexander, a friend of King James I, ignored the French claim to Acadia and settled a group of Scots on Cape

Breton Island, naming the area Nova Scotia. The French
quickly expelled them and the area changed hands frequently until it finally became a British possession in
1713. A visitor to Nova Scotia can still easily see vigorous continuations of the early traditions: Scottish names,
English spoken two centuries later with a Scottish ac-
cent; and Acadian fishermen and farmers who still look
and speak like Frenchmen.

The English-French conflict was most bitter inland,
where it was to have considerable influence on the history of the two nations-to-be. Although many French settlers were engaged in farming, fishing, and the various
occupations of small towns, the heart of the French enterprise was the fur trade, for furs then brought high
prices in the European markets. Obviously, the easiest
way to get furs was to trade for them with the Indians,
although many Frenchmen became trappers themselves
(*coureurs de bois*), traveling great distances in the Indian
canoes to trap and trade for furs. Since Indian tribes
were often at war, the French found themselves taking
sides. From the beginning they sided with the Hurons
against the Iroquois, thus involving themselves in bitter
and bloody wars.

By the middle of the 1640s the French *coureurs* and
missionaries had established ties with Indians as far inland as the Lake Michigan region, well south of what
would become the United States border. This cut deeply
into the fur gathering of the Iroquois who had traded

with the Dutch along the Hudson River. In desperation
they increased the ferocity of their raids on the French
settlements, and New France hung on by a thread with,
in 1663, only about 2,500 persons compared with the
tens of thousands of English, Scottish, Irish, and Dutch
settlers along the coast from Nova Scotia to the Chesapeake Bay region. It seemed that half a century after its
establishment New France might collapse, for France,
torn by war and internal dissension, had been able to
offer its colony little help.

But, as was so often the case, developments in Europe had a profound influence on events in the New
World. Louis XIV decided, upon the death of Cardinal
Mazarin, his chief minister, to make himself the real
ruler of France. New France was placed under direct
royal supervision, new settlers were dispatched as were
soldiers who so severely defeated the Iroquois that they
remained at peace for several years. Most important to
the future of the French-Canadians was Louis' determined immigration policy. The first census was taken in
1666, showing that there were only 3,215 French people
in the colony. Louis not only sent male immigrants but
recruited 1,100 sturdy peasant women (*filles du roi*) to
become wives in the women-short society. In thirty
years the population had risen to more than 15,000. Indeed, the survival of the French-Canadians depended on
these *filles du roi*. It has been estimated that between the
founding of Quebec in 1608 and its capture by the Brit-

ish in 1759 only about 10,000 French emigrated to North America. Since there has been little French emigration since 1759, almost the entire French population of Canada, some five and a half million people, is descended from these early settlers. This does not include a million or so of French-Canadian descent who migrated to New England in the nineteenth century.

This newly invigorated New France embarked on an adventure in which all Canadians, not just those of French descent, can take pride. It was an extraordinary period, those last three decades of the seventeenth century and they are still celebrated in song and legends. The Catholic priests, brave and dedicated men, played an important role as they pushed ever outward to convert the heathen Indians. The names that appear in the history books are those of French noblemen and French and Canadian men of quality, such as the Comte de Palluauet de Frontenac, Robert Cavelier de LaSalle, and Pierre Lemoyne, Sieur d'Iberville. But the men who made this violent and bloody adventure possible were the *coureurs de bois*, fierce men in turn extravagantly friendly and violent, men of enormous appetites who earned huge sums from the furs they gathered by trade and trapping and spent them in wild bouts of roistering, selling, when money ran low, even the fine clothes off their back. When the money was gone, they slipped into the woods, to be gone for months, covering enormous distances on foot through the forests or skimming across lakes and along rivers in canoes. It was a violent and cruel world. They suffered from exhaustion and hunger, partook of the savagery of Indian battles, and not infrequently bore the scars of brutal torture. They were bigger than life, free men who had escaped the restraints of civilization. They both horrified and fascinated the people of the settlements. Their jaunty manner and their quickly spent riches were much more impressive than the dowdy, penny-pinching gentility of the seigniors. As they swaggered around the settlements in their flashy finery, they became the heroes of the community; they became the real nobility of New France. [2]

Though other men had to make the plans and serve as their leaders, it was the *coureurs de bois* who allowed the French to strike swiftly and silently at the English from Hudson Bay far to the north all the way down the Mississippi to the Gulf of Mexico. A few hundreds of men, with their Indian allies, staked out a vast claim not only in what is now Canada but in an immense area of what are now the North Central States and the Mississippi valley. Louis XIV and his lieutenants in North America were not small thinkers. With only 15,000 people in New France, Louis intended to confine the hundreds of thousands of British settlers to a strip along the Atlantic coast by establishing a great inland empire, based on the fur trade, that swept from Montreal all the way to New Orleans.

With France and Britain now at war, the British settlers had all the more reason to counterattack. In the far north the French, under Iberville, took Hudson Bay after traversing great distances on snowshoes, then building canoes and paddling down the spring freshets to fall on the unsuspecting British. But the British struck back. New Englanders hit by sea with punishing raids on the coastal areas of Acadia. And the Iroquois, British allies and bitter enemies of the French, in August 1689 fell on the little town of Lachine, near Montreal, and massacred about sixty inhabitants, the greatest disaster in the history of New France.*

Canadian plans for a naval and military attack on New York collapsed after a series of delays. Their only result was to bring back Frontenac, now nearly seventy, as governor. Frontenac had been governor from 1672 to 1682, pushing an aggressive campaign for the expansion of New France. This involved him in continuing disputes with other French officials who wanted to restrain the fur trade and consolidate New France. These disputes became so bitter that he, as well as his chief opponents, was recalled in disgrace in 1682. However, when the going got rough the French court recognized that the indomitable old man was the only possible choice.

*At this point we shall stop using the terms French and British because most of the men now engaged in these bitter battles were natives or immigrants who had become permanent settlers. On both sides they were developing loyalties to their American homes fully as strong as their loyalties to their home countries. It was still one contested land, but we shall call them Canadians and Americans, for they were now separate peoples even though for nearly a century they would continue to have a common history.

Frontenac brought no reinforcements with him, for France was totally committed to its European conflict with Britain. But age had not withered his fierceness. He realized that a formal expedition was beyond the resources of New France; he relied on the colony's unique strength, the capacity to strike savagely with stunning surprise, a heritage of decades of experience in penetrating the forests for the fur trade. In the winter of 1690, Frontenac sent out three raiding parties — to the New England villages along Casco Bay, to the settlements on the border of New Hampshire and Maine, and to Schenectady in what is now upstate New York.

They moved swiftly, secretly, through the woods and fell suddenly, violently, on the bewildered settlements, killed and burned without restraint, and then straggled in retreat through the snow, sometimes torturing prisoners as they went. This was the instinctive way of New France, for it was a colony half savage and half civilized, reacting inevitably with the primitiveness of the fur trader, the implacability of the religious fanatic, spurred on by the never-ending fear of the Iroquois. They did not see themselves as savages but saw their enemies, the English, as rebels and heretics whose terrible crime had been to strengthen their mortal foes, the Iroquois. They were driven by the need to retaliate and a fanatic zeal to do God's will. [3]

These successful raids had consequences both good and bad. Canadian prestige with the Indians increased. Their alliance with the western Indians confirmed, it was easy for the French-Canadians to open the fur-trade routes to the west. But the very success of the raids goaded the Americans in New England and New York to retaliate. The Americans were far superior in manpower and resources but the colonies had not yet developed the cooperation that nearly a century later would mean independence. The way to defeat New France was obvious: a naval attack on Quebec and an overland attack up the Lake Champlain-Richelieu River route.

A large army was assembled by Major Peter Schuyler at the head of Lake Champlain but for some reason it made only one brief raid. More promising was the naval attack led by Sir William Phips of Massachusetts. In May 1690, his flotilla captured Port Royal in Acadia. Thus encouraged, the Bay State raised a navy of thirty ships and in October they sailed up the St. Lawrence to take Quebec. They seemed to hope they could sail right up the river, the center of New France, and surprise the capital. Obviously that was impossible, yet when Phips arrived at Quebec he sent an officer under a flag of truce to arrange the city's surrender. He must not have known much about Frontenac. Phips's envoy must certainly have been intimidated when the old Count roared at him, "No. I will answer your general only with the mouths of my cannon and the shots of my muskets, that he may learn that a man like me is not to be summoned in this fashion." [4]

Phips landed troops on the tidal flats and furiously

bombarded the fortified cliff-town. His soldiers could do little against the French troops, *coureurs de bois*, and Indians and the fortress was almost invulnerable to bombardment. Within a week Phips perceived the futility of his attack, exchanged prisoners with the indomitable Frontenac, and sailed off to Boston.

New France had held off history — for a time. But her situation was desperate. The Iroquois raids were endless and terrible, disrupting the colony's agriculture, sometimes so badly that food had to be imported all the way from France, with winters sometimes ending in near starvation. The fur trade fluctuated more violently than ever. The supply was uncertain and so were prices. Sometimes there were too few furs and other times they came in such a flood that prices tumbled. Inflation was rampant. Consequently, in Quebec and Versailles an old controversy was revived with increased bitterness: expand or consolidate. For Frontenac, however, there was only one answer: attack, attack, and attack again. His lieutenants, among them Antoine de la Mothe Cadillac, organized the western Indians to strike at the Iroquois. In Acadia the governor and a few French priests and settlers led the Abenaki Indians against the settlers coming north from New England. Most fantastic of all was Iberville. He struck everywhere. He captured Pemaquid on the Maine coast, ravaged the British settlements on Newfoundland, and in Hudson Bay, with a single ship, the *Pelican*, defeated three armed English merchantmen.

Even the old Comte de Frontenac was not content to be a strategist safe in the walled city of Quebec. He personally led his troops against the English and Iroquois of New York. And, in 1696, when he was nearly eighty, he was with the force of two thousand that leveled the strongholds of the Oneidas and Onondagas.

In 1697 England and France temporarily ended their episodic war with the Treaty of Ryswick. The American provisions of the treaty were no mean reward for Frontenac and his Canadians. They regained the whole of Nova Scotia (Acadia) and, with the exception of a post on the Albany River, were allowed to keep all the forts on Hudson Bay. The autumn of 1698 saw the death of the extraordinary Frontenac, who sometimes aped the elegance of the court of his sovereign, Louis XIV, and sometimes danced around an Indian campfire, shouting and waving a tomahawk over his head. As the new century began, the Canadians and their Indian allies made peace with the Iroquois, exchanging belts and planting the tree of peace. To the south, both before and after the treaty with the Iroquois, the French-Canadians tightened their grip on the St. Lawrence and Mississippi river systems. In 1699, the ubiquitous Iberville explored the lower Mississippi and founded a post at Biloxi on the Gulf of Mexico. And, in 1701, in a turnabout of later history, Cadillac added Detroit to the string of forts that anchored the French empire in North America.

France's hold on North America was nonetheless tenuous. Small forts — separated by scores, often hundreds, of miles of wilderness. A handful of men — explorers, adventurers, priests, and *coureurs de bois*. Fragile alliances with Indian tribes. Even so, France might have been able to consolidate this vast empire, changing the course of American and world history and leaving more of a heritage than French names scattered throughout the United States: Detroit, Marquette, Duquesne, Montpelier, Champlain, New Orleans, Beloit. But Louis XIV was too ambitious. He wanted empire both in Europe and America. He could not have both. His new war, the War of the Spanish Succession, drained strength and resources that could have been better used in America. The incredible Iberville wanted to strike at the cities of English America, but France could spare nothing from its European conflict. New France was forced to go on the defensive. Fortunately the peace with the Iroquois held, fighting was not resumed in Hudson Bay, and the vast regions of middle America were not contested by the British — for the moment. But New France disguised its essentially defensive posture with raids on New England and English Canada. The Canadians and their Indian allies massacred the inhabitants of a number of New England towns. When New England tried to retaliate, its success was limited; it was never able to establish successful cooperation with the other colonies or even with mother England itself. In 1709 a colonial army waited all summer near Lake Champlain only to learn that the British fleet that was supposed to attack Quebec had been diverted to the defense of Portugal. Two years later the same commander, Colonel Francis Nicholson, waited in the same place. This time the English fleet came, but it lost eight transports and two supply ships on rocky islands in the Gulf of St. Lawrence. It turned and sailed for home, leaving a thousand bodies floating in the sea.

In America the French-Canadians were holding on, but once again American history was directed by what happened in Europe. The war in Europe had gone badly and France shrewdly made peace with England, separating it from its European allies. France lost Acadia once again but was allowed to keep Cape Breton (the island part of present Nova Scotia). Inland, however, it did not fare so well. It was forced to surrender its recently won sovereignty over the Iroquois and to give up the forts and territories of the Hudson's Bay Company. This Treaty of Utrecht of 1713 was the beginning of the end for New France. It had lost most of its outer defenses in the maritime region, lost Hudson Bay, and in the heart of the continent had been forced to accept the presence of the English on one flank and the Spanish on the other. The final struggle for North America was still to come, but the battle lines were drawn.

France began to prepare for the battle. It had lost most of Acadia, but decided to make Cape Breton Island, which it now called Isle Royale, a bastion of the French presence in the maritime region. An extraordinary fortress was constructed at a splendid harbor near the southeast corner of Cape Breton. Here rose Louisbourg, supposedly the most powerful fortress in all of North America.

Powerful it was, but totally artificial, for its very bricks and stone were carried across the ocean from France and erected on this isolated shore. Inside its wall arose a French community — public buildings, the governor's residence, even a hospital — that was meant to perpetuate the grandeur of France and its civilization. Often there were great men-of-war in the harbor and eventually the garrison reached fourteen hundred men, resplendent in their uniforms of white with blue facings.[5]

But something went immediately wrong with the French plan. The Acadian people simply refused to do what was expected of them, not for the last time, as the English were soon to find out. France had carefully provided in the Treaty of Utrecht that the Acadians, within a year, could move, taking with them their movable belongings. The French invited them to Cape Breton, where they were supposed to establish a substantial farming community that would be the foundation of the French presence in the maritime area. But they simply refused to move; they were not patriots. They did not care who ruled, British or French; they knew that they were not likely to find any better home than the Bay of Fundy region. So the great fortress of Louisbourg remained an isolated redoubt without a viable economic base. Ironically, Louisbourg came to rely on New England traders for most of its provisions. It was supposed to be the citadel of the French against the New Englanders, but ended up contributing to their growing trade and presence in Nova Scotia.

Now it was the turn of the English to be frustrated by the Acadians. They assumed, with some reason, that if the Acadians did not want to be French, they must be willing, if not eager, to become good citizens of the British Empire. But they either refused to pledge their allegiance to His Britannic Majesty or did so with the condition that they be exempt from any wartime services against France and its allies. The English, like the French, were too weak to do much about these stubborn Acadians, so they went about their ways to the frustration of their old rulers and new. Acadia, therefore, was still uncertain territory.

So too was that vast territory sweeping down from Montreal to the Gulf of Mexico. It was essential to the French-Canadians that the area be kept wild as a source of furs. But the British-Americans, pressing ever inward, had to tame the wilds for farms and villages. The forests had to be cleared, which meant there was no place for the beaver or for the native peoples. While the Spanish, far to the south, used the Central and South American Indians as slave labor in their gold and silver mines, the hardy, self-sufficient northern European settlers made the North American Indians obsolete. There was probably no conscious plan to eradicate the peoples whose land they had taken, but the axe and the plow made it inevitable. The fur trader needed the Indian; the farmer, then in America, later in Canada, found him an obstacle.

As the Atlantic settlements continued to expand westward, the final confrontation came closer. The advantages lay with the English. They got cheap cloth from the new British textile mills, dyed scarlet and blue, which the Indians were eager to get in exchange for furs. And New England rum was much cheaper than French brandy. So in addition to clearing the land and establishing villages and towns the British-Americans were increasingly successful in competing with the French-Canadians in the fur trade. In 1722 New York established a fortified trading post at Oswego on Lake Ontario, territory that the French had considered theirs for a century. But the French were not about to give up. With increasing competition to the south from New York and to the north from Hudson Bay, where British ships could sail right to the heart of beaver country, the French turned to the northwest. After voyages of incredible difficulty, they opened up the areas that are now Manitoba and Saskatchewan. They were not economically as strong as the British, but they had long experience in dealing with the Indians. They spoke their languages, lived with them as equals, and offered credit.

The British were more aloof, fewer spoke Indian languages, and they did not offer credit. For a while it seemed as if France had finally stabilized the situation. The production of furs was constant, prices were good, and for several decades after the 1713 Treaty of Utrecht it seemed that New France would prosper, along with Louisiana.

But inevitable trends were already in motion that would determine the history of North America. Though there were great liberal movements in England and France, liberalism made little impact on New France. There the clergy had an iron grip on the culture and it was a gloomy, conservative Catholicism, authoritarian and rigid. Liberalism, though not always triumphant, was older in Britain, and the colonists took its most important product, parliamentary government, to America with them. This explains much of the difference in political development of the two societies. The French-Canadians were cut off from France before the liberal theories and practices of the French Revolution could be exported to the colonies, while the principles of British liberalism (the natural rights of man, etc.) profoundly influenced the Jeffersons, the Adamses, and the Franklins and thus were a major contribution toward the rebellion of the American colonies. Furthermore, the British-American colonies continued their relentless expansion to the north and west. It was clear the French and the British-Americans would inevitably clash again.

New England commerce was thriving, its ships ranging the entire world. As Massachusetts came to regard
Nova Scotia more and more as an important part of its
fishing and commercial system, it decided that Isle Royale (Cape Breton) was an obstacle that had to be removed. The colony's English governor, William Shir-
ley, concluded that the great fortress at Louisbourg had
to be taken. Again, still again, developments in Europe
were crucial. England and France were once more at
war, this time the War of the Austrian Succession. In the
early spring of 1745 an amateur army of about four
thousand New Englanders started for Louisbourg. For
once England and her colonies were able to cooperate
successfully. William Pepperell, the merchant commander of the volunteers, and Peter Warren, commander
of the British fleet, were both competent and cooperative.
The volunteers, being Puritans, prayed a lot and sang
hymns, but they were not reluctant to plunder the
property of non-combatants and drink great quantities
of rum.[6]

But they were good fighters. It did not take long to
capture Louisbourg, for it was not as strong as it looked.
There was dissension among the troops and bad discipline; furthermore, the fortification had been allowed to
fall into disrepair, and it did not have enough supplies to
withstand a determined siege. So on June 17, 1745, the
French colors were lowered for what its conquerors assumed was the last time.

The French, however, were determined to recapture
Louisbourg and the next year sent a mighty armada to
take the citadel, recapture Acadia, and harass the New
England coast. The effort was a total disaster. Plague
infected the fleet and heavy seas dispersed it. What remained of the fleet turned back, sailors dying of the pes-
tilence by the hundreds. In any case the French navy
might not have been strong enough against the growing
seapower of the island England and the maritime New
England. But New France still had its old weapon, the
swift overland strike. In February 1747 the Canadians
and their Indian allies, the Micmacs, fought their way on
snowshoes through wintry drifts and in the midst of a
wild snowstorm fell upon the English at Grand-Pré.
Lacking naval support, however, they could not capture
Louisbourg or even Annapolis. Thus the war came to an
indecisive end in 1748.

The New Englanders were wrong, nevertheless, in
assuming that the French colors would never again fly
over Louisbourg. Although New France had been unsuccessful in war, old France had not. It had won the
latest episode in its endless struggle with England. As
reward it regained Louisbourg. The New Englanders
were outraged, and both sides prepared for the next in-
stallment. Britain decided to settle things once and for
all in Nova Scotia and set about building a mighty fortress, Halifax, at mainland Nova Scotia's magnificent
natural harbor, one of the finest in the world, where,

much later, in two world wars, great convoys would assemble for dangerous voyages across the submarine-infested North Atlantic. Mighty Halifax was to be a counterweight to Louisbourg and the capital of a revitalized Nova Scotia. Twenty-five hundred English settlers were distributed strategically and the Acadians were told that they could not hold out any longer; they had to swear allegiance to the British crown. It was hoped that they would gradually become anglicized and, possibly, even converted to Protestantism.

Nothing, however, concerning Nova Scotia/Acadia was simple. The Micmac Indians harassed the British, while French diplomats argued that the Treaty of Utrecht provided that only the peninsula had been ceded to England and the mainland (now New Brunswick) was still French. While the diplomats talked, the soldiers fortified. Some of the Acadians moved into the French-claimed zone and those who remained on Nova Scotia still refused to take an unqualified oath of allegiance. A final resolution was yet to come.

Inland also, confrontation was coming closer. The colonies of New York, Pennsylvania, and Virginia were expanding westward. France's naval difficulties had weakened the military strength of New France and reduced the goods available for trading with the Indians. Also English intriguers were at work trying to undermine the long-standing French-Indian ties. This enabled the English settlers to push on into Ohio. The French reacted vigorously. They and their Indian allies struck hard at the defecting chiefs and the English influence collapsed.

Dealing with fur-trading rivals was one thing, but dealing with the slow and steady advance of settlers was another. At first the French won. In 1749 a few Englishmen and a greater number of Virginians formed the Ohio Company and were granted a tract of 500,000 acres for development. Four years later a young Virginian, 21-year-old George Washington, was sent out to Fort LeBoeuf to inform the French they had to move; Virginia intended to annex the territory. An emphatic "no" was the answer so Governor Robert Dinwiddie of Virginia tried to take it. In 1754 Washington led a small force of colonials in an attempt to oust the French-Canadians, but the Canadians had strengthened their forces. The two tiny armies met where the Allegheny and Monongahela rivers join to form the Ohio, the site of present-day Pittsburgh. Washington's main body quickly overcame an advance party of the French, but when the Canadians' main force arrived, Washington was soon surrounded. He saw no alternative but to surrender. The French allowed them to go, provided they left the area immediately. When the Virginians left, the French built Fort Duquesne.

All of a sudden, in 1755, the situation exploded. The British colonists decided on a decisive four-prong attack: against Acadia, up along Lake Champlain, against Ni-

agara, and against Fort Duquesne. Only in Acadia did
the British-American campaign succeed. Of more lasting consequence, however, was the campaign against
Fort Duquesne. General Edward Braddock had arrived
in Virginia earlier in the year as commander in chief of
the British forces in America. He decided to crush the
French at Duquesne and set off with 1,400 British regulars and 450 colonials under Washington, now a lieutenant colonel. They were opposed by a mixed force of
only 900 French-Canadians and Indians. But Braddock,
like regular generals before and after him, did not understand guerrilla warfare, which was the only way his foe
knew how to fight. He marched his red-coated regulars
into battle on July 9 as if they were on parade. The
French and Indians refused to accommodate him. Dart-
ing behind trees and giving blood-curdling warwhoops,
they took a terrible toll of the redcoats. Braddock was
mortally wounded and only the skillful retreat organized
by Washington enabled the force to escape annihilation.
Washington's reputation soared. He became the most
famous soldier in the colonies and was thus on the road
to becoming "the father of his country."

Although the campaign against the Canadians in 1755
had only limited success, it marked a new determination
on the part of the British and the colonies, which
showed a capacity for cooperation that the mother country would find less welcome only two decades later.
This determination was most clearly demonstrated by
Colonel Charles Lawrence, governor of Nova Scotia.

After the victory of the New Englanders, he abruptly told the Acadians to take the oath of allegiance or be expelled. Most of them refused, but this time they had come up against someone as stubborn as themselves. He ordered them to gather up their belongings and, on October 8, began sending the Acadians off to the other thirteen colonies. (Nova Scotia has often been called the fourteenth colony and, when the rebellion came, many expected it to join in.) Some 6,000 Acadians were scattered along the Atlantic. Others fled to what are now New Brunswick and Prince Edward Island. Over the years many of them drifted back, their numbers increasing naturally so that there are now about 350,000 French in the Atlantic provinces, most of them Acadians.

France recognized that the situation was serious and in May 1756 sent Louis Joseph, Marquis de Montcalm, a superb soldier, to Quebec. By this time war had again broken out in Europe and, as usual, France and England were on opposing sides. Montcalm might have succeeded in holding New France had it not been for his superior, the governor, Pierre de Rigaud, Marquis de Vaudreuil-Cavagnal. Jealous, the governor interfered with Montcalm's command and was often successful in dividing the army into hostile factions. Despite Vaudreuil, Montcalm started off well, even though he was usually opposed by superior numbers and faced with a foe commanding a much greater population and better resources of all kinds.

Montcalm, in the tradition of New France, took the

offensive. He quickly captured Oswego and in 1757 took Fort William Henry at the head of beautiful Lake George. But by 1758 the tide was turning as William Pitt organized the war effort in London. Louisbourg was taken that summer and the British-Americans began capturing Canadian forts in the interior. The only victory came at Fort Ticonderoga where Montcalm's men shot down the redcoats sent in foolish frontal assault by James Abercromby. Montcalm, with 3,000 men, bested Abercromby's 12,000, killing more than 450 and wounding more than 1,100.

The capture of Louisbourg by Jeffrey Amherst opened the sea approaches of New France and Britain did not hesitate long before seizing the opportunity. In June of 1759 a great armada sailed up the St. Lawrence under General James Wolfe and Admiral Sir Charles Saunders. Montcalm naturally picked the walled city of Quebec for the decisive battle, one of the great battles in world history. Montcalm's army was larger, but Wolfe had a higher proportion of trained regulars and was supported by a mighty naval force.

At Quebec and for some miles upriver, high, steep cliffs afforded a natural defense. But immediately below the city the Beauport flats were an obvious place to land. Montcalm entrenched the shore and placed most of his army there. The British attacked on July 31, with Grenadiers in the van. Montcalm beat them back. There was no further action for a month, but Montcalm knew that

Wolfe would strike again. On September 3 Wolfe began breaking up his camp a few miles downriver from Quebec and soon there was activity some miles upriver. Was Wolfe going to try an attack overland?

Montcalm was not easily diverted, but he was equally concerned about the heights immediately above town. On September 5 he sent a battalion up to the Plains of Abraham to guard the heights. Two days later Governor Vaudreuil ordered the battalion back to Beauport. A few days later someone noticed British army officers across the river carefully surveying the heights on the Quebec side at a cove called Anse au Faulon. Again Montcalm ordered the battalion up to the heights. And again, this time to his face, Vaudreuil countermanded the order. The next day, September 13, he would do something about the defenses of Anse au Foulon.

Before dawn on September 13, at about four o'clock, a sentry heard a noise below him. He called out and someone replied in excellent French that he was from the Queen's Regiment. That seemed plausible, for convoys often came down the river by night to feed Quebec. The boats moved quietly on and moments later were pulled up at the shore at Anse au Foulon. The first man ashore was the lanky General Wolfe. The ruse had worked. How was the sentry to know that a Scottish Highland officer, Simon Fraser, spoke French so well?

Wolfe doubted that the heights could be scaled, but the British soldiers set off as quietly as they could up the

gully of Anse au Foulon. It was too late when Montcalm learned what had happened. Even then Governor
Vaudreuil continued to issue orders that only confused
things. It was not until after eight that Montcalm had
gathered a force outside the city gates. The British army
that could have been so easily thrown back down the
cliffs was waiting for him. Montcalm decided to attack.
Five battalions moved across the Plains of Abraham.
When they came within range of the British and the foe
still did not shoot, they became unnerved. The French
continued on uncertainly and as soon as they got to the
forty paces specified by Wolfe, the British opened up.
The charge was stopped dead. For a moment the French
veterans and the French and Indian irregulars held their
ground but when the British charged, the defenders
broke into disorderly retreat. At this historic moment of
triumph, Wolfe was dying of a rifle shot. And Montcalm, trying to rally his troops, was mortally wounded.
As his black horse walked slowly back to the city gates,
he tried to hold himself up, but he did not live to see the
surrender of Quebec on September 17.

It was all but over for New France. There was still an
army and Canada was not ready to surrender. British
General James Murray's garrison suffered severely during the winter of 1759 and a French attack in the early
spring of 1760 almost recaptured the capital. But when
the ice broke on the St. Lawrence, the British fleet again
sailed up to Quebec. And British and American armies

began to converge on Montreal: Amherst from Lake
Ontario, William Haviland from the south, and Murray
from Quebec. On September 8, 1760 with these armies
massed outside Montreal, Governor Vaudreuil surrendered the entire province of New France. By the Treaty
of Paris in 1763, France ceded all claim to Cape Breton,
Acadia, Canada, and the islands of the St. Lawrence. It
was allowed to retain fishing rights off Newfoundland
and was given (and still has) the two islands of St.
Pierre and Miquelon. It further surrendered its claim to
all the lands east of the Mississippi in what is now the
industrial heartland of the United States.

It was the end of New France, but would it be the end
of the French in North America? Would its culture, its
language, its religion be submerged and eventually absorbed by a triumphant British America?

The future ordeals of French Canada might be terrible, but its society had grown stronger in the struggle of
the past century and a half. It was deeply rooted in the
soil, was nurtured and sustained by a powerful religious
faith and a distinctive language; above all, it had shown
a great determination to survive. With this determination, with these attributes of religion and culture and
devotion to the soil, French Canada might survive. And
if it did survive, amidst a population predominantly British, it would create the fundamental social and cultural,
even spiritual division in the life of British North America, one that would be supremely difficult to reconcile. [7]

2

A Continent Divided

FOR TWO CENTURIES France and Britain had contended for northern North America. In 1760 the issue seemed settled for good. There would be one great British colony, from the Mississippi to the Atlantic, from the St. Lawrence to Hudson Bay and far to the west. The various strands of history — British, French, coastal, maritime, inland, north, south — would all converge. There would be just one history now. Canadian history and American history would become just North American history. Gradually, the French would be absorbed and the great

British Empire would be greater than ever. But it was not to be. The American Revolution was not far off and though its greatest effect, of course, was the birth of the United States, it had a profound influence on the history of Canada and no little influence on the preservation of the French presence in North America. Here we see intertwined, not for the last time, the two great themes of Canadian history: the influence of the United States and the French-English conflict.

First we must look at Nova Scotia, that difficult colony that never seemed to do what was expected of it, and then at Quebec, which has long since superseded Nova Scotia as the most perplexing part of Canada. In the famous Royal Proclamation of October 1763, both areas were dealt with. New France was renamed Quebec Province and large territories, to the northwest and the southwest, were sheared off, leaving the province with roughly the boundaries it has now. The territory to the southwest, below the Ottawa River and between the Appalachians and the Mississippi, was to be kept as a vast Indian reserve with white settlement prohibited until the tribes were pacified and treaties could be negotiated.

Britain wanted immigration to move north into Quebec and northeast into Nova Scotia. This desire was fulfilled in the case of Nova Scotia. Almost immediately New Englanders began to move to Nova Scotia, which, because of the forced removal of the Acadians, was almost empty. They soon established fruitful farms and profitable fisheries. The population increased from about 2,000 in 1763 to 17,000 in 1775, the eve of the American Revolution. The New Englanders often came in groups and brought their institutions with them: town meeting government and Congregational churches. It might seem that Nova Scotia would become another part of New England. To be sure, New Englanders dominated it numerically and certainly it had a New England flavor, but it was a bit different, too. The people were now physically isolated from New England, and Nova Scotia, because of the magnificent harbor at Halifax, had strong and direct ties with England. The officials and merchants pretty much ran the province, since the hinterland, with its New England democratic traditions, had little access to the capital.

Most of the officials of New France departed, for they were mostly natives of France, and the British put in their own officials. More important in the long run was the fact that a number of English and Scottish merchants arrived in the province, eventually taking over the fur trade that had been the lifeblood of New France. From this they naturally gained economic dominance in the region and have continued to hold it for two centuries. This dominance of the economy of French Canada by English-speaking people has been a bitter source of conflict in recent decades.

Other than the merchants, there was only limited immigration of English speakers to the province and it soon became clear to a succession of military governors that Quebec was not soon going to become English and Protestant. This was not particularly bothersome to the military governors, however, because the first three were conservatives and great believers in authority. Since French society was much the same, the governors were quite pleased. A French conservative society was much easier to govern than the impossible democrats of the thirteen colonies. So they did not try as hard as they might have to convert the French Catholics into good English Protestants. With things getting a bit touchy in the thirteen colonies, it hardly seemed the time to upset Quebec's stability by trying to enforce drastic changes. The powerful French-Canadian clergy was pleased to go along, particularly since they had long felt more allegiance to Rome than to Versailles.

As the thirteen colonies edged closer to rebellion, London found its vast American empire difficult to govern. It decided that it would be easier to restore to Quebec the great area between the Ohio and the Ottawa rivers, thus reestablishing the fur-trading empire headquartered in Montreal. This was embodied in the Quebec Act of 1774 which also established a special oath so Roman Catholics could participate in the government. It also confirmed the feudal landholding system, established the old French law in civil suits, and gave the Church the right to collect the tithes.

This was a last straw for the thirteen colonies. The

Boston Tea Party had already taken place and the British Parliament was beginning to crack down on the colonists. Thus, they saw the Quebec Act with its pro-Catholic provisions and, worst of all, the awarding to Canada of land they regarded as theirs, as part of a hostile program. This was hardly surprising. The rebellious colonists were by now suspicious of anything the Crown did and they had long been conditioned to think of Quebec as an enemy. Thus British policy toward Canada contributed to the American Revolution.

But if the Americans had a real degree of hostility toward Quebec, they also had a sense of community. The thirteen colonies, Nova Scotia, and Quebec were all subject peoples and the Americans assumed on the eve of the Revolution that all subject peoples in North America wanted to be free. And since the French-Canadians had been enemies of the British for a century and a half, the Americans assumed they were instinctive allies. Thus, in October 1774, a month after it had opened in Philadelphia, the Continental Congress sent an open invitation to the people of Quebec to elect a delegation to represent them at Philadelphia. When that invitation failed to get an immediate response, Doctor John Brown of Massachusetts was sent to make a personal appeal. He soon wrote back to Boston, "There is no prospect of Canada sending Delegates to the Continental Congress."[1]

Quebec and Nova Scotia had their grievances, but

there were good reasons for their staying out of the war. Although the Quebeckers had little reason to love the British, the British had been smart enough to allow French society to continue little changed, secure in its language, culture, and religion. And if the British had been the enemies of New France so had the colonists of New York and New England. There was little choice between them, and the Quebeckers knew where they stood with Britain. As for Nova Scotia, it continued on its own stubborn course. By 1775 it was about three-quarters New England in population. While the provincial assembly swore its loyalty to King George, illegal town meetings gave secret support to New England. Though the great Halifax merchants continued to support the Crown out of self-interest, others traded with New England. The decisive fact was geography. Nova Scotia was, in those days of the sail, distant from New England and vulnerable to the powerful British navy. So the New England Nova Scotians did what their Acadian predecessors had done: they tried to remain neutral. The Nova Scotian dilemma was well expressed by the inhabitants of Yarmouth in 1775.

We do all of us profess to be true Friends & Loyal Subjects to George our King. We were almost all of us born in New England, we have Fathers, Brothers & Sisters in that Country, divided betwixt natural affection to our nearest relations, and good Faith and Friendship to our King and Country, we want to know, if we may be permitted at this time to live in a peaceable State, as we look on that to be the only situation in which we with our Wives and Children, can be in any tolerable degree safe.[2]

Reasonable as this may have seemed to the Nova Scotians, it did not seem at all reasonable to the fire-brands of New England. In 1776 revolutionary forces tried vainly to capture Fort Cumberland on the Isthmus of Chinecto and all during the war there were repeated efforts to persuade Congress or the Massachusetts General Court to attack. But these efforts failed for the reason advanced by Washington in rejecting a proposal to attack Windsor on the Bay of Fundy:

It might, perhaps, be easy with the Force proposed to make an Incursion into the Province . . . but the same Force must Continue to produce any lasting effect. As to furnishing vessels of Force, you, Gent[n], will anticipate me, in pointing out our Weakness and the Enemy's Strength at Sea. There would be great Danger that, with the best preparation we could make, they would fall an easy prey either to the Men of War on that Station, or some who would be detached from Boston. . . .[3]

If the British navy protected Nova Scotia, there was no similar protection for Quebec Province. Governor Carleton had only a few scattered troops. So the French and Indian Wars were reenacted. In April 1775 the Massachusetts Committee of Safety authorized Benedict Arnold to raise a force of four hundred men in Western

Massachusetts to attack Fort Ticonderoga on Lake Champlain. The fort was important strategically; also it held a great supply of artillery and other weapons. While Arnold was raising the men, he learned that Ethan Allen was assembling a force, the famous Green Mountain Boys, to attack Fort Ticonderoga himself. Arnold hurried to Castleton, Vermont, tried without success to take command, and decided to accompany Allen anyway. The Americans surprised the British garrison of forty-two men on the morning of May 10th. The British quickly surrendered to Allen, whose force outnumbered them two to one. Within a few days Crown Point, north of Ticonderoga, was seized as was, temporarily, St. John's in what is now Canada.

More ambitious invasion plans became necessary with the news that Governor Carleton was raising a Canadian army. The Continental Congress authorized General Philip Schuyler to strike first and seize any points important for the defense of the colonies. He raised a force of about a thousand men and started north from Ticonderoga on August 28. On September 6 he laid siege to St. John's, now garrisoned by about six hundred British and Canadian troops. But Schuyler became ill and was forced to turn over his command to Brigadier General Richard Montgomery. St. John's surrendered on November 2.

Governor Carleton then moved with his small force to the defense of Quebec City. He had failed to recruit more than a few French-Canadians into his militia. Several hundred of them joined the Americans, but most remained neutral. With no opposition, Montgomery occupied Montreal on November 13, almost capturing Carleton a few days later.

In the meantime, Benedict Arnold, with Washington's approval, had raised in Massachusetts a force of about 1,100 volunteers. They marched north, on September 12, to Fort Western (Augusta), Maine. Then on the 24th they pushed on through difficult country seldom penetrated by white men. The terrain was so difficult and supplies so short that Arnold had to send back one of his four battalions. After more than a month on foot, Arnold reached the St. Lawrence opposite Quebec on November 8. It had been an extraordinary trek. Arnold crossed the river on November 13 and on December 3 he was joined by Montgomery, who had marched down from Montreal with three hundred men. Again, the future of Canada would hinge on a battle at Quebec City. And again it looked as if the walled city would be taken. Carleton had only a motley defense force of a few hundred regulars, militia, and Indians. The Americans had nearly a thousand men. But appearances were deceptive. The Americans had no artillery, they were poorly supplied, and the early Canadian winter had set in. The only possibility for the Americans was a swift, violent attack. It came, like Wolfe's in the pre-dawn hours, on New Year's Eve and it was accompanied by a wild snowstorm. This time, however, the defenders prevailed. The attack was a disaster. Montgomery was killed, Arnold wounded, a hundred men killed or wounded, and another three hundred captured. Nonetheless, Arnold maintained a weak blockade until the spring thaw enabled the British navy to sail upriver.

The Americans withdrew, but that was not the end of Canada as an important factor in the Revolutionary War. Both sides recognized the importance of Lake Champlain. Whoever held it held an enormous advantage. Both Arnold and Carleton began to assemble fleets but it was not until October 11, 1776 that they clashed. Arnold's flotilla had eighty-three guns, Carleton's eighty-seven. More important was the quality of the crews. Arnold's was a motley, pickup lot while Carleton's were experienced sailors. That made the difference and in a seven-hour battle most of Arnold's inland navy was crippled. Those of his boats that escaped were attacked again two days later and Arnold's flotilla was eliminated as a fighting force. Carleton recaptured Crown Point on November 3 but decided winter was too near for an assault on Fort Ticonderoga.

It was now 1777, a crucial year for the fortunes of the rebellious colonies. British General John Burgoyne (Gentleman Johnny) got London's approval for a three-pronged attack: a push southward down Lake Champlain and the upper Hudson Valley; an auxiliary attack through the Mohawk Valley from Oswego; and another strong

push up the Hudson River from New York City. Thus
Canada was to be the base of what was meant to
be a knockout blow against New York and New
England.

Burgoyne began his campaign on June 17, leaving
St. John's with about 7,700 men, British and German
mercenary regulars, Canadians and Indians. He had
138 pieces of artillery and a huge baggage train. The
campaign began well and the Americans evacuated Fort
Ticonderoga on July 5 when their position became un-
tenable. But by the beginning of August things began
to go badly for Burgoyne. Despite his huge baggage
train, he was running short of supplies and he was being
harassed on all sides, guerrilla fashion, by American
militiamen. Their numbers swelled daily as word spread
through New York and New England of the atrocities
committed by Burgoyne's Indians. Despite heavy casualties, Burgoyne pushed south, finally stalling just below
Saratoga. He sent urgent calls for help, but the British
push up the Hudson ran out of steam at Kingston, well
below the spot where Burgoyne was facing defeat. By
the beginning of October Burgoyne began to retreat
back toward Canada but now the American forces under
General Horatio Gates, with Benedict Arnold continuing
to play an important role, were so strong that Burgoyne
could go neither forward nor back. On October 13, surrounded by a force three times the size of his, Burgoyne
asked for the terms of surrender. On October 17 Bur-

goyne's 5,700 men, all that were left, laid down their arms. They were to be marched back to Boston and then sent back to Britain under the pledge that they would not serve again in the American war. That was the end of Canada's substantial participation in the Revolutionary War. But it was much more than that. It was an incalculable boost to the morale of the patriots and it caused France, which was already unofficially helping the rebels, to recognize America's independence and join in a formal alliance, pledging to give armed support to the rebels until the Revolution was won.

From this point on what was to become Canada would cease to be a major influence on what was to become the United States. But the reverse was far from true. From this point on the United States would have a great, sometimes crucial, influence on Canada. That would become obvious in 1783 when Britain and the new United States signed a peace treaty. Canada remained a colony. It had expressed no interest in 1777 when the thirteen colonies to the south had agreed to the Articles of Confederation which stated, "Canada, acceding to the Confederation and joining in the measures of the United States, shall be admitted into, and entitled to all the advantages of the Union."[4]

Having spurned, not for the last time, an opportunity to become part of the United States, Canada found to its horror that vast territories, which it had always considered its own, were to go to the United States. Although Great

Britain had clearly been defeated along the Atlantic and along the Hudson-Lake Champlain pathway to Montreal, it was still the single most powerful nation in the world. Deep within the American continent, it still controlled the forts and posts which dominated that great triangular territory between the Ohio and Mississippi rivers. This region, as we have seen, had long been under the influence of the *coureurs de bois* and the priests and had been governed, to the extent anyone could govern it, from Montreal. Furthermore, none of the thirteen colonies had ever possessed that area and just before the Revolution Britain had rejoined that area to the Province of Quebec. Most important, Britain still held it.

When the treaty negotiations began, Britain's negotiators were not very well informed on North American geography; they wanted to be generous with the determined Americans to try to separate them from Britain's age-old enemies, the French; but mostly Britain was just weary of the struggle and not prepared to carry it on in negotiations. Also the American negotiators, John Adams, John Jay, and Benjamin Franklin, were determined and skillful. At first they suggested that the best way to a reconciliation would be to have no northern boundaries at all, which meant ceding all of Canada to the United States. The British negotiators were interested, but that was too much for the British Cabinet. Then the Americans offered what are now the United States-Canadian boundaries between the ocean and the Mississippi. Anything beyond that could be taken up later. Britain accepted. One can scarcely blame the Canadian historian Donald Creighton for sounding a bit cross when he contends that Britain ceded to the United States, with a few casual strokes of the pen, a great empire that the colonists along the St. Lawrence had built with more than a century of effort. He argues that the Western Indians, whose territory the English had guaranteed, were betrayed, and that the fur traders, who had sustained Canada from the start, had been ignored. The unity of the region, built on the trade in furs, was broken at a time when it was still intact.[5]

The American negotiators also gained the right for New England fishermen to fish within the three-mile territorial limit of maritime Canada and to dry and cure their fish on unsettled shores of British North America.

3

Canada and the New Nation

WE SHALL CALL that land to the north of the United
States Canada although, strictly speaking, Canada was
solely what was then the Province of Quebec, roughly
what are now the provinces of Quebec and Ontario.
Properly speaking, it was British North America, although by a twist of history, much of British North
America spoke French. Thus, at the end of the Revolutionary War there were several colonies to the north:
Canada, Nova Scotia, and Newfoundland. Canada was
mainly French-speaking, Nova Scotia was mainly popu-

lated by New Englanders, and Newfoundland was much as it had long been, an island colony of people from the British Isles who worked hard and lived frugally. There was very little thought that these colonies, so distant in geography and so disparate in makeup, would become one nation.

The American victory not only changed the geography of Canada but its aftermath meant a change in populations as well. America took land and gave people. These were the Loyalists who, during the Revolution, had remained loyal to the British crown. There were all degrees of Loyalists, from those who quietly refused to aid the rebel cause, to those who fled their lands, sometimes leaving the country, sometimes flocking to British-held areas, to those who joined Loyalist military units that fought alongside the British. Those who fled usually had their land and property confiscated. Those who remained were subject to all sorts of indignities, from surveillance to robbery to personal attack.

As the war drew to an end, thousands of Loyalists from downstate New York and Pennsylvania, plus smaller numbers from other colonies, gathered in New York City, the last large port held by the British. No one knows exactly how many Loyalists there were — estimates range from something over fifty thousand to perhaps one hundred thousand. About a third, including many of the wealthy, returned to England. Others went to Florida or the West Indies. The largest number, about

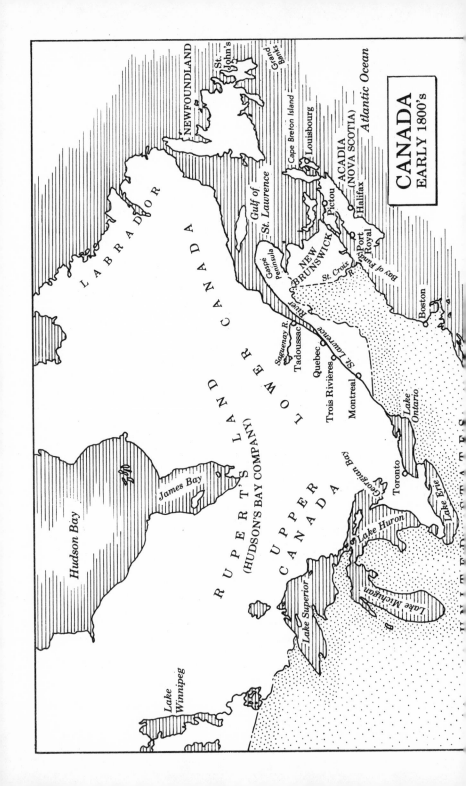

thirty thousand, went to Nova Scotia. Most of these were from settled areas and it was difficult for them to carry on the pioneering life necessary in Nova Scotia. Some settled on Cape Breton Island and some on peninsular Nova Scotia but most went to what is now New Brunswick. The Loyalists were not comfortable among the New Englanders of Nova Scotia. They preferred to be among themselves and to govern themselves. Therefore in 1784 the new province of New Brunswick was carved out of Nova Scotia.

After the war the British negotiators tried to establish certain rights for the Loyalists. But it was difficult. In the first place the Articles of Confederation conferred little power on the central government. All the American negotiators could do was promise that Congress would "earnestly recommend" that the states restore the rights and property of both British residents and Loyalists who had not taken arms against the revolution. As for those who had taken up arms, it was to be recommended that they be allowed to return for a year to try to regain their property. Neither the states nor the people paid much attention to the recommendations of Congress. Loyalists found it uncomfortable, even dangerous, to remain. Particularly in the upper New York State region where the Loyalists and their Indian allies had fought bitter and bloody battles with the rebels was it impossible for them to remain. Most of the Loyalists from that region, mainly farmers, went north and northwest after

the war. Some of them went to the area now known as
the Eastern Townships of Quebec Province, between
the St. Lawrence and the United States border. That area
thus has English names although the population in later
years became largely French-speaking. Others — even
more — went north and west to what is now Ontario.

The first years after the war were not tranquil along
the new American-Canadian frontier. There were
boundary disputes, but more important was the continued presence of British soldiers in the forts in the old
fur-trading area. The British used the treatment of the
Loyalists as a pretext. They weren't trying to hold on to
the land; they hoped to be able to prevent a revival of
the Indian wars. But the Indians saw this presence as a
promise of help against the encroachments of the hated
Americans. And the Montreal fur traders dreamed of
somehow recapturing their commercial empire. The
Americans, of course, saw the British presence as du-
plicity.

But mainly the Americans and Canadians were concerned with more immediate matters. In Quebec there
was the beginning of the English-French problem that
plagues Canada to this day. With substantial numbers of
Loyalist immigrants, the circumstances had changed.
No longer was it almost exclusively — with the exception
of the merchants and bankers — a French area. The new
immigrants had proved their loyalty to the British crown
and they demanded their rights as British subjects. They

wanted English laws and English political institutions. The French-Canadians, of course, felt that their survival depended on a continuation of the old ways permitted by the British conquerors after the fall of Quebec City in 1759.

There was no easy solution. What the twenty thousand English speakers demanded, the one hundred thousand French speakers were not prepared to accept. The entire area of Quebec was one economically but finally London decided that it must be broken in two, something fairly easily done since most of the French speakers lived from Montreal downriver and most of the English speakers west of the Ottawa River. Thus, in 1791, the provinces of Upper Canada (roughly present-day Ontario) and Lower Canada (roughly present-day Quebec) were established. Since the English speakers wanted a voice in their government and since it was in the British tradition that they have one, London quickly devised a system. However, Britain had learned from its experience with the American colonies. It did not want the Canadian provinces to have so much self-government that they would soon demand more. Authority was divided among a governor, an appointed executive council, an appointed legislative council, and an elective assembly. It was more conservative than the American system, but then Canadian society — the Loyalists in Upper Canada and the French in Lower Canada — was also more conservative. The new institutions reinforced the politically conservative, socially hierarchical character of the two Canadas.

Soon after Upper Canada was established, it became a fertile ground for those Americans moving ever westward in search of the good life. They filled the gaps in the Loyalist settlements around Lake Ontario and on the peninsula between lakes Erie and Huron. By the eve of the War of 1812, Upper Canada had a population of about eighty thousand, most of whom were recent immigrants from America, with no particular Loyalist sentiment. More concerned with land than politics, these immigrants easily settled into the Canadian political system which, although more authoritarian, was not so very different from what they had known.

In Lower Canada, however, the French-Canadians soon caught onto parliamentary government and, from the beginning, were a clear majority in the elected assembly. But it was different in the other branches of government. The appointed governor was British, of course, and there were English-speaking majorities in the appointed executive and legislative councils. Britain was consciously keeping the French speakers from getting a large measure of power in their own province, especially after 1793 when Britain and France again went to war. Thus the English-French division began to widen.

While this was going on in the two Canadas, the fur trade was making its last effort, and a magnificent effort it was. With the Hudson's Bay Company controlling the trapping grounds to the north and American settlers moving into the great triangle formed by the Mississippi and Ohio rivers, the only direction in which the Montreal fur traders could seek the beaver was to the northwest. The traders were largely Scots but the men who penetrated the vast distances of the Northwest were descendants of the *coureurs de bois*, tough French-Canadians who could bear the terrible physical burdens and the great danger. The Nor'westers, like the great seamen of centuries before, were also seeking a Northwest Passage, not by sea but by the mighty rivers that traversed the wilderness. Most famous of the explorers of those days in the early 1790s was Alexander Mackenzie. Together with four French-Canadians, a German, and a few Indians, he discovered the river that now bears his name. In frail bark canoes they journeyed down the river to the Arctic Ocean. Even such an adventure was not enough for the young Scotsman. He wanted to reach the Pacific where, it was said, Russian fur traders prospered. In 1793, with only a few men, some veterans of his previous exploit, he tried another river, the Peace, whose wild waters belied its name. He fought the river, then the great cliffs of the canyon through which it roared. The mountains behind him, he struck overland, arriving at Dean Channel on the Pacific on July 22, 1793, the first man to reach the Pacific overland.

While Mackenzie and his intrepid companions were

demonstrating the course of future Canadian development, there was a last hope that Montreal could hold
onto its fur empire below the border. English troops still
held those posts and now London was awakening to the
knowledge of what it had given away. Canadian fur
traders said they had lost from a half to two-thirds of
their trade. The Indians, long-time allies of the British,
were crying betrayal and the United States was providing a pretext for the continuance of British control. The
posts would be handed over, a righteous Britain said,
when the United States had done justice to the Loyalists
and had arranged the payment of pre-Revolutionary
debts, both as provided for in the peace treaty. This
encouraged the Indians and their long-time partners the
fur traders, both of whom shared the same hope: that the
relentless advance of the American frontiersmen could
be halted, saving the hunting grounds of the Indian and
the preserve of the fur trader.

Not surprisingly the Indians rose against the Americans and not surprisingly the Americans blamed the
British, who quite possibly were not entirely blameless.
But no one can blame the Indians for resisting. They
had come to learn the bitter lesson that the Americans
wanted their land and would take it, often making solemn
treaties with Indian chiefs that were soon broken. Two
American armies were sent against the Indians and both
were defeated. The British began to hope they could
restore their credit with the Indians. They proposed

themselves as mediators, suggesting that a neutral Indian state be established between the American and British claims, the state, needless to say, being on the American side of the new boundary. The Americans were not enthusiastic about this modification of the Paris Treaty of 1783 and sent "Mad Anthony" Wayne to deal with the Indians. Wayne defeated them at the Battle of Fallen Timbers, and with this defeat, it was obvious the redcoats would soon have to leave. This was arranged by John Jay, Chief Justice of the United States, who was sent by President Washington as a special envoy. The last redcoats marched out of Indian territory by the middle of 1796.

The War of 1812 was just over the horizon but before we consider that strange war, with its lasting impact on Canada and its transient effect on the United States, we must look again, as often we will, at the developing schism between English speakers and French. Changes were taking place in Lower Canada and, as always, change was unsettling to the ruling classes. Among the French, the *seigneurs* and the upper clergy continued to support British authority. But from the rural *habitants* a new class of professionals was springing up, often lawyers and journalists who had struggled for an education. Many of them turned to politics and when they discovered that appointive office was closed to them, going either to English speakers or to French speakers, much more conservative than themselves, they became restive.

To the anger of the English-Canadians, these young French-Canadians often cited English law and traditions as the basis for their demands for a larger share of the government. When this share was withheld, they, not surprisingly, began to see *les Anglo-Saxons*, a term that was now common in French Canada, as enemies of their people. The disagreement came to a head in the period between 1807 and 1810 with the governor, Sir James Craig, violently opposed to the French nationalists. He moved suddenly to dissolve the assembly, seized the nationalist newspaper, and arrested a number of French-Canadians. He then went so far as to recommend to London that any form of representative government that permitted French-Canadians to control the assembly should be abolished. This was too much for London, which recalled Craig and sent out a more conciliatory governor on the eve of the War of 1812. Perhaps Britain felt it had enough on its hands without stirring up Lower Canada.

Historians still cannot agree on the reasons why the United States declared war on Britain in June 1812. There were a number of factors but it is nearly impossible to determine which were paramount. Relations between the United States and its parent had been deteriorating for a number of years. Britain and France were engaged in the last, titanic episode in their centuries-long conflict. Napoleon controlled much of the European continent and prevented Britain from trading with most of it. Britain, for its part, blockaded Europe. In 1807 the British man-of-war *Leopard* stopped the American frigate *Chesapeake* on the high seas and took off four men to serve in the British navy. This outraged American public opinion and there was great pressure on President Thomas Jefferson to declare war immediately. He decided instead on an embargo on trade with Britain, hoping that in the middle of its great war with Napoleon it would not want to cope with such a difficulty. But the embargo failed to force Britain to recognize American rights on the high seas while causing a bitter dispute within the United States. The New England merchants, shipowners, and shipbuilders were enraged by the embargo. They wanted to trade with England and it did not make them any happier to see this trade go to their old rivals in the maritime provinces north of the border.

Nonetheless, most of the United States wanted to do something about Britain. Inland, the growing West felt the loss of markets caused by the British blockade and everyone was convinced that the British were behind the violent Indian attacks as the Shawnee chief Tecumseh and his fanatical brother, the Prophet, tried to rally the tribes for one last determined stand against the advancing Americans. And, no doubt, there were those who wanted finally to conquer Canada. This is not as unlikely as it may seem now, for from the middle of the eighteenth century until the beginning of the twentieth, one could always find prominent men who believed that one way or another, perhaps in war, perhaps in peace, Canada would be joined into – to use Jefferson's words – the great American "empire of liberty."[1]

Canada could hardly look upon such a war with confidence. While the British navy could, if it could be spared from the European blockade, protect the maritime provinces, Lower Canada was populated by a restive mass of French-Canadians and Upper Canada was largely populated by American immigrants. And there were less than five thousand British regulars in the northern provinces. It seemed like just the right time for the United States to go to war because Britain was entirely pre-occupied with the last phases of its struggle with Napoleon.

Canada seemed ripe for the taking. Why then wasn't it taken? In the first place, the United States, despite its overwhelming advantage in population – some seven and a half million against less than half a million – had severe weaknesses. Men of New England, the region closest to Canada, refused to serve in the army, bought British treasury notes instead of American bonds, and happily traded with New Brunswick and Nova Scotia. Furthermore, despite the fact that a large proportion of the nation had been calling for war for five years and that the government had been considering it all those years, the regular army had been reduced, forcing the United States to rely on poorly trained militia. And the

United States, which had provided so many superb generals in the Revolutionary War, seemed to specialize in incompetents during this one.

The war was fought in two main theaters, the Atlantic and the upper St. Lawrence and lakes Ontario and Erie. At sea the tiny American navy could hardly hope to stand up against the British, although American frigates occasionally did well in single combat. Thus the strategy was to concentrate on British merchantmen. In this the Americans did well, taking some fifteen hundred prizes in three years. But the American merchant fleet suffered badly, too, and little by little the powerful British navy swept the seas clean of U.S. fighting ships.

Inland things were supposed to be better. In the summer of 1812 three American armies assembled for what was assumed to be the easy conquest of Canada. The campaign was an utter fiasco. With 2,200 men under him General William Hull crossed into Canada from Detroit on July 12, tarried about four weeks, and then hurried back to Detroit, reportedly fearful that Tecumseh's Indians would massacre women and children. For some reason he surrendered to General William Brock without firing a shot. He was later court-martialed and sentenced to death for cowardice and neglect of duty, but the sentence was remitted because of his good record in the Revolutionary War.

That would not have been so bad if General Stephen Van Rensselaer had struck north of the border near Niagara at the same time that Brock was involved with the timid General Hull. But Van Rensselaer was somehow delayed and did not take the offensive until October 16, allowing Brock plenty of time to get over from Detroit. The Americans seized Queenston Heights but the 600-man force was crushed by the thousand defenders because the New York militia refused to reinforce them, claiming that the terms of their military service did not require that they leave the state. Van Rensselaer turned over his command to General Alexander Smyth, a regular army officer. His attempt to cross the Niagara River on November 28 was so feeble that he was relieved of his command and dropped from the army. The biggest American force was under General Henry Dearborn. It was supposed to advance on Montreal while Smyth drove across the Niagara River. Smyth's failure did not make much difference, for Dearborn's militia refused to cross the Canadian border. So Dearborn had to turn back.

President Madison obviously had to do something about the army. Steps were taken to reinvigorate it and one of the most important was the appointment of the famed Indian fighter, William Henry Harrison, as a major general. Harrison, at the head of 10,000 men, was ordered to retake Detroit. He engaged in some bloody battles with the British and his old Indian foe, Tecumseh, and suffered heavy losses. He found he could not take Detroit as long as the British controlled Lake Erie. That job was given to a 28-year-old captain, Oliver Hazard Perry, who on the 10th of September, 1813, won one of the most famous naval battles in American history. When the British guns were silenced, Perry sent a message familiar to millions of American school children: "We have met the enemy and they are ours." Perry's historic victory allowed Harrison to move north into Upper Canada where, on October 5, 1813, he won the Battle of the Thames River. The battle had lasting consequences for in it the great Indian chief Tecumseh was slain. This led to the collapse of the Indian confederacy and caused the Indians to desert the British cause. Harrison's victory had made the northwestern frontier secure and did much to add to the fame that later took him to the White House.

That year 1813 also saw another attempt to take Montreal. This, too, failed. The British forces were much stronger than they were the year before and the generals in charge of the two-pronged American attack disliked each other so that cooperation was difficult. Neither James Wilkinson nor Wade Hampton pushed his attack with much resolution and the drive fizzled out long before it reached Montreal, both men going into winter quarters. At year's end Lord Castlereagh had grown disillusioned with Britain's chance of winning the senseless war and on November 4 sent an official letter to Secretary of State James Monroe, proposing direct negotiations to end the conflict. President Madison was eager to end the war, especially since it had not been going well.

But diplomacy took months in those days when trans-

Atlantic messages traveled by sailing ship. Madison accepted promptly and by February the U.S. Senate had confirmed a peace commission. While letters moved slowly back and forth across the Atlantic, the Flemish town of Ghent was chosen as the negotiating site and talks began on August 8, 1814, almost nine months after Castlereagh proposed them.

During all this time the war went on. The American army had improved, but its improvement was more than compensated for on the British side by the fact that the defeat of Napoleon on April 6, 1814, allowed Britain to send large numbers of battle-proven troops to North America. Until they arrived, however, the Americans took the offensive. In early July Major General Jacob Brown and Brigadier General Winfield T. Scott moved north across the Niagara River to seize Fort Erie, across the border from Buffalo. Two days later the main British force of about 1,500 men drew themselves up on a plain about a mile north of the Chippewa River. They were attacked by Scott's brigade of 1,300 men. It was the only battle in the entire war in which approximately equal numbers of regular troops met without one side or the other having the advantage of position. The battle was sharp and short. When it was over, the British had lost 137 men compared to Scott's 48. But once again the lack of cooperation bedeviled the Americans. Their first real chance for an important victory vanished when Commodore Isaac Chauncey, the American naval commander on Lake Ontario, refused to cooperate in planning a campaign to conquer Upper Canada.

Once again the Americans had to retreat. They fell back on Fort Erie. A strong British force, that included six heavy siege guns, launched a determined attack on August 15, but it was thrown back with heavy losses. The British, however, kept up their heavy bombardment until a powerful sortie from the fort destroyed the artillery pieces. With that the British withdrew as did the Americans a couple of months later.

By this time the British veterans of the Duke of Wellington's army were arriving on this side of the Atlantic. Britain planned a mighty three-pronged attack: south from Canada along the traditional Lake Champlain invasion route; from the sea at Chesapeake Bay; and the third, also by sea, against New Orleans. All this was planned to take place even while the peace negotiators were meeting at Ghent. Obviously Britain was determined to hand its negotiators a series of victories that might well enable them to get back some of what was lost in the Revolutionary War. But this was not a war in which things went well for either side for long.

Up in Canada General Sir George Prevost had a powerful army of 11,000 British veterans supported by a fleet of 4 ships and 12 gunboats with 90 guns and about 800 men. The American commander, Alexander Macomb, had only about 3,300 men, a mixed force of regulars and militia. The only hope of withstanding the

British army was for the Americans to hold onto Lake Champlain. The American naval commander was a 30-year-old captain, Thomas Macdonough. His fleet was about the same size as the British: 4 ships and 10 gunboats with 86 guns and about 850 men. The only significant difference was that the American guns, although more powerful, had a shorter range.

While Prevost drove the much smaller American army before him, Macdonough carefully placed his flotilla in a narrow channel across the bay from Plattsburgh. By September 6 Prevost had driven Macomb's tiny army into a heavily defended position just below Plattsburgh. There he waited for the British flotilla. It arrived on September 11 and immediately engaged Macdonough's force in the Battle of Lake Champlain. For two hours it appeared that the British would win, opening the entire Hudson valley to Prevost's army. But in the final minutes Macdonough bore down with his flagship, *Saratoga*, on the British flagship, *Confiance*. The *Saratoga*'s broadsides caused the *Confiance* to strike her flag. The United States had won undisputed control of the vital Lake Champlain and with it ended Britain's last threat from Canada. Prevost, who for some reason had not used his shore batteries to support his naval guns, turned toward Canada. Many of his troops deserted and he left behind huge quantities of supplies.

Although that ended the major phase of the War of 1812, the Canadian phase, it is necessary to examine quickly the results of the two other prongs of the British attack. One was enormously successful, although it had no lasting influence, and the other was not only a disaster but took place after the Peace of Ghent had been signed in Europe. The British success, of course, was the attack up the Chesapeake Bay. It was intended to be a diversion, to draw American strength from the north to benefit the British drive from Canada. But while the primary drive failed, the diversion was one of the black moments in American history. The British force of four thousand veterans under General Robert Ross left France on June 27 and arrived at Chesapeake Bay in mid-August. Its orders were "to destroy and lay waste such towns and districts upon the coast as you may find assailable." [2]

General Ross interpreted his orders broadly — and boldly. The British squadron sailed up the Chesapeake to the mouth of the Patuxent River where Commodore Joshua Barney had a small flotilla of gunboats. Barney blew up his boats on August 22 to prevent their falling into British hands. He took his four hundred men and five 24-pound guns overland to Washington. There the defense of the capital was in the hands of one of the incompetent generals who had survived the shakeup of the army. Perhaps Washington seemed so safe that it was thought to be a waste of a competent general to keep him so far from the fighting near the Canadian frontier. But General William H. Winder did the best he could. He rallied from nearby states several thousand militiamen and decided to meet the invaders near Bladensburg, now a Maryland suburb of Washington. When, on August 24, the battle became imminent Winder hurried out to take command, followed by President Madison and most of the Cabinet, much the way Presidents often attend the Army-Navy football game. An interesting spectacle it must have been; enjoyable it could not have been. Three thousand British soldiers routed the seven thousand Americans. The most effective American soldiers were Commodore Barney's sailors. They were given the task of covering the American retreat and for half an hour they held off the British forces, now swollen to four thousand men, inflicting three casualties for every one they suffered.

The retreat turned into a rout and the army simply deserted Washington. The British marched in unopposed and put the torch to the Capitol, the White House, and most of the government buildings — purportedly retaliation for the American burning of York (Toronto) earlier in the war. From Washington the British turned toward Baltimore but there they failed. While the British were occupied with Washington, Baltimore had erected strong defenses and had assembled a larger defense force. The unsuccessful attack was most notable for inspiring a witness to the bombardment of Fort McHenry, Francis Scott Key, to write the verses to the National Anthem, "The Star Spangled Banner." By September 14 the British gave up their attempt to take Baltimore and the next month sailed out of Chesapeake Bay for Jamaica.

The war presumably ended on Christmas Eve 1814 with the signing of the Treaty of Ghent but unfortunately the peace treaty was on one side of the Atlantic while the fighting was on the other. Thus, in December another British fleet from Jamaica was sailing through the Gulf of Mexico, determined to capture New Orleans. The vast Louisiana Territory was now American, having been purchased by Jefferson from Napoleon in 1803, doubling United States territory. The British wanted to take control of the mouth of the Mississippi and its strategic river basin. This thrust was also a surprise, but the army commander in the Southwest was no incompetent. He was Andrew Jackson, a blooded veteran of the Indian wars.

The British headed directly for New Orleans with Jackson harassing them, then withdrawing to a point five miles from the city. He used a dry, shallow canal to erect breastworks between a cypress swamp and the east bank of the Mississippi, thus making it impossible for the more numerous enemy to outflank him. The first engagement was by artillery and the British found themselves outgunned. They would have to attack with infantry. A week later Sir Edward Pakenham had his reinforcements and on January 8 he decided on a frontal assault. British regulars in close ranks charged the American breastworks, 5,300 attackers against 4,500 defenders. The Americans not only had the advantage of position but many of them were Kentuckians and Tennesseeans, deadly shots with their long rifles. The British and their generals were brave; Pakenham and two other general officers were killed. But it was a foolish assault. There and on the west bank, where an associated battle was fought, the British lost 2,036 men killed and wounded while the American casualties were 8 killed and 13 wounded. The British withdrew, the war was over in fact as well as on paper, and Andrew Jackson was a national hero who would end up in the White House.

What did the war add up to? Almost precisely nothing. The Treaty of Ghent did not discuss, even in passing, the issues that caused the United States to declare war. There was nothing about search and impressment on the high seas, nothing about military control of the Great Lakes region, nothing about the Indians. All that was definite was that the accepted boundaries remained as before the war and a number of disputes were to be settled in future negotiations. Other than preserving the still-young United States, the war had little lasting influence on the nation. But it did have a long-lived influence on Canada.

The War of 1812 has sometimes been termed Canada's war of independence, for if the United States had won, instead of the war's ending in an inconclusive draw, it almost certainly would have taken much, if not all, of what is now Canada. And the war bred in Canadians a suspicion of the United States that was slow to die. " . . . most Canadians agreed with the opinion expressed by the Quebec *Gazette* in 1845, that 'no country can be safe in the vicinity of the United States.'"[3] (This was a more prosaic wording than the Mexican saying: "So far from God and so close to the United States.")

This suspicion lasted throughout the entire nineteenth century, fueled not only by specific incidents but by public statements of various prominent American spokesmen who declared that one day Canada would enjoy the benefits of American democracy.

> . . . there were at least six occasions between 1814 and 1867 when war seemed a possibility. In 1838 the sympathizers of the Canadian rebels, Mackenzie and Papineau, tried to create trouble by mounting invasions from American territory. In 1839 militia from Maine and New Brunswick clashed on a disputed borderland in "the war of Pork and Beans," which fortunately ended in comedy and compromise. In 1846 hostilities seemed very near when Britain and the United States clashed over Oregon, and President Polk, intoxicated with dreams of Manifest Destiny, issued the war cry "Fifty-four forty or fight" in support of his claim to the whole of the Pacific Coast as far as the southern boundary of Alaska at 54°40'. In 1859 there was again an uncomfortable season in the west, over the disputed San Juan Islands in the Gulf of Georgia, while on at least two occasions in the 1860s the resentment of the northern states over Britain's recognition of the Confederacy as a belligerent brought the shadow of war over the Canadas and the Maritimes.[4]

Although, as mentioned earlier, American statesmen

are constantly and proudly proclaiming the fact that the Canadian-American frontier is the longest undefended border in the world, it was not always so. All through the nineteenth century all Canadian military preparations were based on the assumption that the United States would be the enemy. As late as 1933, Defence Scheme No. 1 of the Canadian general staff was "a war plan the general assumption of which was that there existed a clear and present danger upon the Dominion of Canada by the armed forces of the United States."[5]

But if there was suspicion of the United States, there was also admiration of the dynamic society south of the border. All through Canadian history there are those — fewer in recent years — who have advocated annexation to the United States or closer economic ties even than those that exist. And millions of Canadians have emigrated to the United States. Both these strains, suspicion and admiration, will be touched on again in these pages.

4

Toward Confederation

ONLY SLOWLY IN the years after the War of 1812 did the idea grow of one Canada from sea to sea. Although the United States had been a unified country for decades, in the early and middle years of the nineteenth century Canadians did not think of themselves as being one. The Newfoundlanders and Nova Scotians and the people of New Brunswick regarded themselves as distinctive subjects of the British Empire. And they and the English-speaking peoples of Upper Canada were divided by the hundreds of miles of French-speaking Lower Canada.

But similar forces were at work on both sides of the border. Immigrants poured into both countries, mostly from the British Isles: Irish fleeing crop failures; Scottish crofters (tenant farmers) thrown off their land by the landlords; Englishmen fleeing bad economic conditions. Many of the new North Americans moved west to where there was land for the taking. In Canada the immigration drastically changed the ethnic composition of the colonies. The French, although still by far most numerous in Lower Canada, became outnumbered by English speakers in Upper Canada.

In Upper Canada development was fairly orderly. It was a relatively new area where farming and forestry were merely a matter of growth and expansion. But Lower Canada was an old area whose economy had depended on the fur trade. After the war the Americans chased Canadian fur traders out of what had been their richest grounds. And the Montreal fur traders had been unable to keep their grip on the fur areas in the Northwest. They had been forced to merge with and be absorbed by the more strategically located Hudson's Bay Company. The Montreal business men had to find something new. Fortunately the forests and the farms provided goods for which there was a ready market in Britain and the rest of Europe. Lumber, wheat, and flour were in the early stages of becoming great industries and Montreal was ready to exploit them, using what had always been the region's great resource, the St. Lawrence River.

Montreal was also hoping to become the shipping center for the products of the growing American Middle West. New York was, as always, a stiff competitor, and with the completion of the Erie Canal in 1825 the competition became even sharper. What was necessary was the extension of the St. Lawrence route westward. That way was blocked, however, by the rapids at and above Montreal and by the Niagara Falls. Lower Canada would have to build canals, too. But there was no money. Already in Britain there was grumbling that British North America was costing the taxpayers at home more than it was worth. The only other source of sums large enough was the elective assembly. The merchants were, however, as we noted earlier, English speakers. The governor was friendly and they were well represented in the appointed executive and legislative councils, but as members of a small English-speaking minority had very little representation in the elected assembly. The English speakers had economic control and a large measure of political control but not as much as they needed. The French speakers had virtually no share of the economic control of the province and only a small part of the political control. Paradoxically, that small part was in the elected assembly where, by British tradition, money bills had to be initiated.

The situation was anything but simple throughout the 1820s and 30s. There were some French-Canadians who supported the plans of the merchants and some English speakers, notably Irish immigrants, who supported the French position. And there were developments in Upper Canada that would cause American-Canadian tensions to get thrown into the hopper, again mixing the two chief themes of this book: American-Canadian relations and English-French separatism.

To try to untangle these complexities, it is necessary first to return to Lower Canada. The leader there was Louis Joseph Papineau who, perhaps paradoxically, regarded himself as a constitutionalist in the English tradition. He, a French-Canadian, was playing the role played by English parliamentarians in the past. He believed that elected legislatures were the heart of government and that the executive should be responsive to the wishes of the people. Here the advocates of authoritarian government were the English merchants, just the opposite role from what they had played at home. After a while, however, Papineau and his followers became convinced that there was more than a political and constitutional struggle involved; they were sure a campaign was under way to destroy the French-Canadian culture.

Indeed, in 1822, the merchants had persuaded London to make an attempt to unite Upper and Lower Canada in such a way that the French-Canadians would be outvoted in the elected assembly and their language cease to be used in official records and eventually in assembly debates. Vigorous protests caused this plan to be shelved but the French were not reassured since the governor during most of the 1820s, Lord Dalhousie, was entirely in sympathy with the English party.

By the 1830s tensions were even higher, with both sides more frantic than ever. Papineau became more extreme in his demands, causing him to lose his more moderate supporters, both French and English. But he did not lose his support in the countryside, where bad harvests, undependable markets, and rural overpopulation had made the *habitants* restive and susceptible to nationalist appeals. The English party, on the other hand, was more convinced than ever that the French — in their view backward, illiterate, and unenterprising — were unfit to hold political power. This view, which has not entirely vanished in English Canada, is a basic cause for the hostility of French-Canadians toward English-Canadians.*

While tensions were not surprising in Lower Canada, one would not expect great internal tensions in the more homogeneous Upper Canada. There, as in Lower Canada, the conflict was constitutional but the division was partly one of class, partly philosophical, rather than ethnic. Just as the English merchants dominated the ap-

*A distinction must be made here. Although with French-speaking Canadians language and nationality are largely synonymous, that is not so with English-speaking Canadians. Over the years distinctions have faded among Canadians of English, Irish, Scottish, and American descent and they are generally regarded as English-Canadians. They constitute about 44% of the population. French descendants — almost all of whom speak French — make up about 30%. About 25% of the population — most of whom speak English — are descendants of neither of the "founding peoples."

pointed councils in Lower Canada, an oligarchy, later to be called the "Family Compact," dominated them in Upper Canada. The members of the Family Compact, some old Loyalists from the United States and their descendants, and some recent arrivals from Britain, were more English than the English. They wanted Upper Canada to be more like Britain and argued that American immigrants, who composed such a large proportion of the colony's population, could not be trusted.

The Family Compact wanted to strengthen the Church of England, develop schools along British lines, encourage British immigration and discourage American. They went so far as to persuade the colonial government, at a time when immigration regulations were less stringent than now, to declare American-born settlers aliens, unable to vote or hold office until naturalized. This not only jeopardized the political rights of the many American-born but perhaps also their land titles. By the end of the 1820s the conservative leaders were confronted by a strong protest movement that was well represented in the elected assembly, sometimes controlling it.

Among the reformers who demanded a broader participation in government were those who cited the arguments of natural rights used by the American rebels and who pointed at American political practices as being desirable. This, of course, enabled the conservatives to accuse them of being pro-American, an effective tactic considering that the memories of the War of 1812 were still so fresh.

By the mid-1830s the reformers in Upper Canada were almost as frustrated as those in Lower Canada. Indeed, the reformers in both colonies were in close touch and trying to coordinate their activities. But there were differences. Papineau, although republican in viewpoint, was more a nationalist leader than a political theorist. The radical reform leader in Upper Canada, however, William Lyon Mackenzie, was a political philosopher who combined in his program both American democracy and socialism.

In both colonies the conflict erupted into violence in 1837. In Lower Canada it was more or less accidental. Papineau's *patriotes* held a demonstration in Montreal on November 6. They clashed with members of the Doric Club, a fraternal club that drew its membership from the pro-English, anti-French minority. The Doric Club drove the *patriotes* out into the suburbs. A few days later Papineau and some colleagues left town to escape the situation, only to have the government jump to the conclusion that they had gone to raise the French countryside in general revolt. On November 16 the government issued warrants for the arrest of Papineau and his lieutenants. This did spark armed resistance and there were a few armed clashes until British regulars ended resistance. Papineau himself quickly scuttled across the border.

The time when the few British troops in Upper Canada were down in Lower Canada to end the *patriotes'* little rebellion seemed to Mackenzie just right for starting one in Upper Canada. Mackenzie had recently lost a bitterly fought election in which the governor had openly taken the side of the Family Compact, calling all reformers, moderates and radicals alike, agents of American republicanism. Mackenzie concluded that only armed force could remove the oligarchy and he went about organizing rebellion. But planning was botched and by the time the rebellion was scheduled to begin in early December the army was back from Lower Canada. A few rifle shots were fired and a few cannon shot and the rebellion was over. Mackenzie, like Papineau, fled into the United States.

Both rebellions were over, but their aftereffects caused great tension along the Canadian-American border. Mackenzie and a number of his countrymen took refuge in the United States, and their arrival aroused support for "Canadian freedom." All along the border, Patriot Societies and Hunters' Lodges were formed, which made no secret of their purpose: to invade Canada. Hundreds of Americans and Canadian refugees were formed into military units. They were armed and drilled on American soil; they gathered supplies and boats, and they made little or no effort to conceal their activities.[1]

The loyalist Canadians, for their part, helped the pot boil by destroying, in American waters, a steamer that had been supplying a Patriot army based on an island on the Canadian side of the Niagara River.

The "generals," some American and some Canadian, squabbled and planned more than they fought and there were only half a dozen or so substantial raids into Canada during 1838. The United States government did not encourage these raids but the state militia were often openly sympathetic to the Canadian rebels and the local courts simply would not convict violators of the neutrality laws. In any case, the incursions were easily stopped by Canadian forces and eventually degenerated into banditry marked by murder, arson, and robbery. The whole affair certainly did little to promote the idea of republicanism in Canada and did a great deal to revive the hostile memories of the War of 1812.

The political turmoil in Upper and Lower Canada had brought things pretty much to a standstill and thousands of farmers were leaving the provinces for the United States. Just at that crucial moment Lord Durham was sent from London to study the situation. He arrived in May 1838 and left in November, after a quarrel with the British government caused him to resign and return home. But his study was intensive enough to result in what has been termed one of the great state papers of the British Empire, *Report on the Affairs of British North America*, which came out early in 1839.

Durham, needless to say, was bombarded with advice as soon as he arrived. He listened to everyone and quickly reached conclusions, which he presented in the vigorous language of his report. His conclusions were, in a sense, paradoxical, for in dealing with the government of the Canadas he had been influenced by the reformers, led by Robert Baldwin. On dealing with the French-Canadians, however, he had been influenced by the Conservatives, the English party. As to government, he was soon convinced that British North America would prosper only if it had internal self-government. Foreign affairs and defense should remain British responsibilities, he argued, but the governor should rely on advisers who had the support of a majority of the elected branch of the assembly. This would require

> . . . no change in the principles of government, no invention of a new constitutional theory, to supply the remedy which would, in my opinion, completely remove the existing political disorders. It needs but to follow out consistently the principles of the British constitution. . . . We are not now to consider the policy of establishing representative government in the North American colonies. That has been irrevocably done. . . .[2]

He wanted, in short, to have British cabinet government practiced in its North American colonies, not only in the two Canadas but in Nova Scotia, New Brunswick, Prince Edward Island, and Newfoundland as well.

This was clearly a progressive recommendation, while his proposal for dealing with the French-Canadians was just as clearly not. Durham accepted almost entirely the view of the English merchants of Montreal that the French-Canadians were an obstacle to the commercial development of the St. Lawrence route, that they were backward, narrow, and reactionary. This led to the paradoxical conclusion:

> . . . despite the fact that Durham was committed to the grant of self-government to British North America, he was equally convinced that the French-Canadians could not be entrusted with political power. Because they were the majority in the most populous province, this view might appear to pose an insoluble dilemma, but Durham found an answer in his plan for the union of the two provinces. When the English population of Lower Canada was added to that of Upper Canada, the total would outnumber the French-Canadians, who would thus be politically impotent and, in time, led to give up their vain ambition of maintaining a separate nationality in North America. As French culture had all but disappeared in Louisiana, so, Durham argued, it should be encouraged to disappear along the shores of the St. Lawrence. There was no place for it in North America where civilization was to be Anglo-American in tone.[3]

Durham thought that all the colonies of British North America should be joined together somehow but refrained from making this recommendation as he became aware of the resistance to union in the Atlantic colonies. The idea of union of Upper and Lower Canada found favor in London more quickly than his proposal for internal home-rule. How, London wondered, could a governor serve two masters, the Crown and the local elected assembly. So internal self-government was postponed for a time, but in 1840 the British Parliament established, to be effective the following year, the united Province of Canada. The union did not, however, follow the lines suggested by Lord Durham. He had wanted it arranged so that the English population of Lower Canada added to that of Upper would give the English control of the united province. At first it did not work that way. Canada East (Lower) and Canada West (Upper) were given the same representation in the united assembly. Whether or not the combined English population was greater than the French, French control of Canada East was assured. This was all right with Canada West until its population exceeded that of its neighbor. Then, as we shall see, they protested vigorously.

During the 1840s there were a series of developments that had lasting effect on the future of Canada. Boundary settlements with the United States in 1842 and 1846 set the boundaries as they are today. Although this removed some of the Canadian-U.S. tension, the Canadians continued to be suspicious of their southern neighbor, which was growing so much faster. This meant that they continued to look to Britain for protection, thus retarding any movement toward independence. While the North American colonies continued to look toward Britain, there was great sentiment in Britain to reduce the economic burden caused by the colonies. This led to sharp reductions in the preferences enjoyed by Canadian wheat, flour, and timber. Combined with a terrible depression in the home country, this caused the colonies, of necessity, to turn to increased trade with the United States, thus establishing the north-south pull toward absorption that Canada has had to fight to this day. Also during the 1840s the idea of home-rule grew irresistibly, with Nova Scotia receiving it in 1848, Prince Edward Island in 1851, New Brunswick in 1854, and Newfoundland in 1855. Nevertheless, these were still independent colonies with little idea of joining together. The impetus toward federation came as a result of conflict between the English-Canadians and the French-Canadians in the nominally united Province of Canada.

5

One Dominion — Almost

WITH THE UNION of Upper and Lower Canada and the achievement of internal self-government in the North American colonies, an irresistible movement toward federation had begun, even if it was not recognized at first. The impetus came from the two factors that constantly reappear in these pages: the English-French conflict and renewed concern about the United States.

The first was the more important. Union of Upper and Lower Canada was a reality, but it had not worked out the way Lord Durham and the Montreal merchants had expected. The French simply refused to be submerged. They looked for allies among the English and soon found them in the Reformers of Canada West led by Robert Baldwin, for the Family Compact, the Conservatives of the former Upper Canada, were natural allies of the conservative merchants of Lower Canada. As often in politics, mutual enemies make mutual friends. The Reformers and the French, led by Louis Hippolyte Lafontaine, cooperated, the first time that English and French worked together in friendly and constructive fashion.

In the early days of Canadian union the British governors adopted a lofty, above-the-partisan-battle approach that brought them the support of both Reformers and Conservatives from both halves of the colony. But the Reformers soon discovered that while the governors were happy to have their support, they weren't so happy with their advice. So in the fall of 1843 both the English and the French Reformers withdrew their support for the governor. This led to bitter political struggles in which the governor, Sir Charles Bagot (and later Sir Charles Metcalfe), increasingly identified himself with the Conservatives.

We can never know where this increasingly acrimonious struggle might have led, for in 1846 there was a change in the government in London and a new governor, Lord Elgin, was sent to Canada. He acted under the supervision of a new Colonial Secretary, Earl Grey, a brother-in-law and admirer of Lord Durham. Grey's views were clear. As he wrote to Sir John Harvey, the governor of Nova Scotia:

> The object with which I recommend you this course is that of making it apparent that any transfer which may take place of political power from the hands of one party in the province to another is the result not of an act of yours but of the wishes of the people themselves. . . it cannot be too distinctly acknowledged that it is neither possible nor desirable to carry on the government of any of the British provinces in North America in opposition to the opinion of the inhabitants.[1]

In the elections of 1847 in both Nova Scotia and Canada the wishes of the people were made clear. They wanted Reformers to form the government. In Nova Scotia the transfer from Conservatives to Reformers went smoothly, but not so in Canada. Particularly in Canada East the English Montreal merchants saw their scheme collapsing. Because of their association with the Reformers, the French-Canadians were prominent in the new government. The merchants' anger was increased by, and perhaps based on, the breakdown in trans-Atlantic trade caused by the end of preferential tariffs and the depression in England. Finally, on April 25, 1849, the rage and frustration of the Montreal merchants broke out. As Lord Elgin was carried by carriage away from the legislature, English-speaking Montrealers pelted him with trash. The mob's passions increased as time went on and after dark, bearing torches, they broke into the parliament building, smashed furniture, and finally set the building ablaze.

Twelve years before it had been Papineau and his radicals who had resorted to violence. Now violence came from the very bastion of English conservatism. Nor did that outburst lance the abscess of English frustration. In the fall more than a thousand Montreal merchants and politicians signed a manifesto calling for the annexation of Canada to the United States. They argued that Canada could achieve material progress only by joining the United States. Furthermore, such a move would end the threat of French rule. But the manifesto received virtually no support.

Although the Montreal English were in despair, their plight was only temporary, for the overwhelming force of the English-speaking immigrants would soon change the situation as would increased investment capital from Britain. Early in the 1840s canal construction had begun that would improve the St. Lawrence route to the west—not mere barge canals like the St. Lawrence's chief competitor, the Erie, but ship canals. By the end of the 1840s capital was beginning to stimulate railroad construction. The railroads represented the east-west attraction that would eventually tie Canada together from coast to coast. The increased trade with the United States represented the north-south pull.

This north-south pull was interpreted in two entirely different ways. Lord Elgin, now governor-general of British North America, believed that it would lessen the possibility of annexation to the United States. He thought it would bring prosperity and thus undercut the argument of the Montreal merchants that prosperity required annexation. But there were others who argued, and still do, that trade with the United States brought the two sides closer together, with the United States, the more powerful, necessarily the chief beneficiary.

The British government came down entirely on the side of increased trade with the United States. As well as having an almost religious belief in free trade, Britain hoped that increased prosperity would allow its colonies to pay a higher proportion of the North American defense budget, about which British politicians had been complaining for years. This, of course, demonstrates that both Britain and its colonies were still wary of the United States, for who else could pose a threat to British North America? By the early 1850s there was strong pressure in British North America for reciprocal trade with the United States. At first the United States was not much interested but then the Great Lakes states came to like the idea of an alternate trade route. More important, New Englanders wanted access to the inshore fishing grounds of the Maritime Provinces. Thus a Reciprocity Treaty was passed easily by the American Congress in 1854, the Northerners believing it was the first step toward annexation, which would bring the Union several more anti-slavery states. The Southerners, on the other hand, accepted Lord Elgin's view that increased trade would lessen the possibility of annexation.

The Reciprocity Treaty was the high point of a trend

toward closer U.S.-B.N.A. ties. Interestingly, it was at this time that B.N.A. adopted the decimal system used for American money, departing from the pounds, shillings, and pence used in Britain until 1971. But there was a counter-trend as well: an increase in the construction of east-west railways. Private funds for the Grand Trunk Railway were soon exhausted and the Canadian provincial government took over the financial burden. This required a new source of funds so the province decided to put a tariff on manufactured goods. This was not a violation of the treaty with the United States, which covered only natural goods, but many in the United States saw it as a violation of the spirit of the treaty. Britain was even angrier about the tariff, but the provincial finance minister, A. T. Galt, warned London it could not interfere. Since this was clearly as much a foreign as a domestic matter, Galt's assertion indicated that the province of Canada was taking on greater powers.

At this same time Canada was running out of farmland in both its eastern and western halves. From the east French-Canadians were crossing the border to work in the New England mills and from the west farmers were leaving for the U.S. midwest. By the 1850s Canada had no frontier in the sense that the United States still had one. There were, to be sure, abundant lands to the northwest but they were far distant and under the control of the fur-trading Hudson's Bay Company which certainly was not going to encourage settlement. The To-

ronto *Globe* might proclaim that "Providence has en-
trusted us with the building up of a great northern people, fit to cope with our neighbors of the United States,
and to advance step by step with them in the march of
civilization,"[2] but others saw the situation as ominous.
Although those vast regions were under British sovereignty, there was fear that American settlers might simply seize the land, settle it, and eventually annex it to
the United States. There was certainly a basis for such a
fear since exactly that had happened in Texas. Nor had
the United States hesitated to grab enormous territories
in the Mexican provinces of California and New Mexico. Without westward expansion, these Canadians rea-
soned, their economy and society would fail and thus
Canada would inevitably be absorbed by a United States
that had never made a secret of its desire to rule the entire continent.

Nonetheless, there was still not sufficient impetus for
a determined Canadian push westward. Additional impetus would soon come, however, from the increasingly
sensitive internal situation of the presumably united
province of Canada. It became more difficult than ever
to reconcile the interests of English Canada West and
French Canada East. Everything was tried. There was
an equal number of Cabinet members from each half of
the province, even a two-headed prime ministership.
This awkward system lasted a while but began to break
down under the pressure of increased population in

Canada West. The flow of English-speaking immigrants to that area was greater than even the extraordinary natural increase of the French-Canadians in Canada East. In 1830 the population of what would be Canada West was half that of Canada East. In 1851 Canada West had 952,000 persons compared to 890,000 and in 1861 it was up to 1,396,000 compared to 1,112,000. Canada West had been content with equal representation when it had a smaller population than that of Canada East. Now the West insisted on proportional representation, while the East demanded guarantees that the French nation would be preserved. And then, as now, the more extreme French nationalists demanded separatism. French-Canadians, conservatives, moderates, or radicals, then and now, have never been able to forget that many English speakers regarded them as an inferior people. With the long memories that usually characterize a beleaguered group, they could not forget that Lord Durham had proclaimed that they had neither a history nor a literature and should be made into Englishmen for their own good.[3] The French-Canadians could not be expected to accept the statement that they had no history, considering that the most dramatic era in Canadian history occurred during the time that Canada was still New France.

A way toward the temporary solution of the English-French conflict (there has yet to be a permanent solution) began to emerge in the middle 1850s with John A.

Macdonald, perhaps the greatest figure in Canadian history, as the chief architect. The parties in Canada were loose associations of French and English speakers whose party loyalties were uncertain at best. The Conservative party leader, Macdonald, formed a coalition with a French-Canadian group headed by George E. Cartier. The new party was given the marvelously ambiguous name Liberal-Conservative. The French component of the new party was larger than the entire party of French liberals, the *Parti Rouge* led by A. A. Dorion.

We saw earlier that the French politicians, headed by Lafontaine, had cooperated with the Reformers, led by Baldwin. But that was a temporary alliance, based on the fact that they had a common enemy, the English Conservatives, who had no use for the French. Macdonald, unlike the earlier Conservative leaders, was both broad-minded and intelligent. He recognized that no party could have political success in the united province unless it could gain substantial French support. And he saw that was possible only by acknowledging the unquenchable French determination to survive as a people.

The French, for their part, as we saw earlier, were mainly a conservative people, close to the land, respectful of authority and obedient to the Roman Catholic Church. The Church had broken with Papineau's *Patriotes* in 1837 and now the French-Canadian clergy eagerly followed the lead of Pope Pius IX, who was a strong reactionary. They had long been distrustful of the rise of liberalism in France and perhaps were not very unhappy to have been cut off from its influence by the British conquest of New France in 1759-60. Thus, it is not so surprising that the French clergy and peasants became the political allies of English Protestant businessmen.

As the 1850s came to a close, Macdonald and a number of other statesmen, from the Maritime Provinces as well as from Canada, began to think more seriously of federation. To Canada, particularly, it seemed a way out of its English-French dilemma. Each side recognized that it needed the other economically but they could not seem to get along together politically. The Liberals proposed a local federation: separate Upper and Lower Canadas that would work together under some loose arrangement. The Conservatives, particularly those with major business interests, proposed a federation of all of British North America: the two Canadas separate but joined with the Maritimes.

Nothing happened for a while, but it was generally accepted that the strong tradition of provincial separatism would prevail over the idea of federation.

In the new decade, the 60s, developments in the United States, as in 1812, increased the sentiment for union not only in British North America but in Britain as well. The Civil War broke out in the United States. Britain, although at first it had no real fears, decided to bolster its forces in Canada. Then there seemed a real chance of

war when on November 8, 1861 the captain of the
Northern warship *San Jacinto* stopped the British mail
packet *Trent* and by force removed two Confederate
agents bound for London. Britain protested loudly, for
its domination of the seas had been affronted. Any satisfactory response from the United States was slow in
coming. The North rejoiced for it had seen nothing but
setbacks in the first months of the war. Furthermore, the
North was angry that Britain had recognized the Confederacy as a belligerent and angry that Britain did not
support the anti-slavery cause that the North believed all
free men should support. On both sides there was sharp
talk of war.

This, needless to say, alarmed the Canadians, who
began to fear another American invasion. Britain rushed
fifteen thousand reinforcements across the ocean and
during the harsh Canadian winter sledged troops from
Halifax across the snowy forests of New Brunswick and
Canada East to Quebec and Montreal. In the Northern
states there was angry muttering in the newspapers that
after the war the United States would see to those British colonies up north. In response anti-American, that is
to say, anti-Northern, sentiment began to spread through
British North America. Fortifications were erected at
various places along both sides of the frontier.

The fear of an American invasion faded as Northern
armies became more involved in the terrible struggle
with the South. Nevertheless, it was obvious that British

North America had to set its own house in order, if not to contend with an eventual invasion at least to prepare itself for a period of uncomfortable relations with its giant southern neighbor. Thus, the idea of union gained new momentum. Concern over future relations with the United States was added to the need to find a way out of the political difficulties of the two Canadas and the need to establish conditions for the economic growth of British North America.

An opportunity to push the idea of union presented itself in 1864. In the two Canadas John A. Macdonald, the Conservative, and George Brown, the Reformer, had decided that a federation of some sort was essential to end the political and economic problems of their region. Macdonald preferred a federation of all British North America and Brown a federation of the two Canadas. They agreed to form a coalition government—neither side had been able to remain in power long—and seek a federation. First, a general federation would be tried and, if that were not possible, a local federation.

In August the Canadians heard of a meeting to be held in Charlottetown, Prince Edward Island. The Maritime Provinces, Nova Scotia, New Brunswick, and Prince Edward Island were also considering some sort of amalgamation for defense and trade purposes. The Canadians asked if they could attend and were invited. When they arrived on the morning of September 1, they found that the meeting had already started without them.

This was not a promising beginning but as soon as the Maritimers heard of their arrival, they postponed their conference in order to hear the Canadians. The Canadian proposal, whatever its dangers, was magnificent. The idea of one great nation sweeping across a mighty continent from sea to sea made the scheme of a Maritime federation, for which there had been no strong feeling anyway, seem pretty small. The meeting wandered from Charlottetown to Halifax, then St. John and Fredericton, finally dispersing with the agreement to meet at Quebec on October 10 to consider the Canadian plan for a federation of all British North America.

Quebec was where Canadian history had its start, and where Canada as a single continental nation was to be born. But the idea of the birth was easier to come by than its realization. The same colonies that met at Charlottetown were again represented: Canada West, Canada East, Prince Edward Island, New Brunswick, Nova Scotia, plus a two-man delegation from Newfoundland. Each colony would constitute a province with Canada East and Canada West again being divided to assure the French-Canadians that in their own province their culture, religion, and language would be preserved in the face of the increased Anglo-Saxon majority that would come with federation. Both the central and the provincial government would be responsible to the people but one area was left unclear, a problem that has plagued Canada to this day — the exact limits of provincial authority were not defined.

The delegates quickly decided on a bicameral national legislature. The lower house, later to become the House of Commons, would be elected directly on the basis of population. The upper house, later the Senate, was to be something like the House of Lords, with members to be appointed by the federal government. It was designed to counterweight to some extent the advantage the more populous two Canadas would have in the lower house. After some haggling, the delegates decided to divide the Senate into three equal parts, each based on a geographical region: the Maritimes and the two Canadas. Each would have twenty-four seats. Within the Maritimes Nova Scotia and New Brunswick would each have ten and Prince Edward Island four. Newfoundland, which made no commitment to join, would be allotted four when and if she joined, to be balanced by four for British Columbia and the Northwest. Finally, everyone voted for the plan except Prince Edward Island which stubbornly, and vainly, held out for five seats.

Although the conference was not a total success, the Canadians were satisfied. They soon found, however, that their optimism was premature. The proposal was promptly ratified by the people of Canada West and, despite some muttering, by those of Canada East. But the story was entirely different in the Maritimes. The Canadian leaders learned to their horror that the Maritime delegates did not have the support of their people. The very idea of federation was opposed by many who, for geographical and economic reasons, looked to the sea,

away from mainland Canada, for trade with Britain and
Europe and the growing United States. No one was surprised that Prince Edward Island was not eager to join
the federation. But in Nova Scotia opinion against federation was so strong that the government would not put it
before the legislature. And in New Brunswick, absolutely crucial because it provided the link between the other
Maritime Provinces and the two Canadas, the pro-fed-
eration government was defeated in an election in January 1865.

The great dream seemed about to die when once
again the United States revived it. Relations between the
United States and British North America became worse.
They had been bad all during the Civil War because of
British support of the South. The militarily irrelevant but
dramatic raid on St. Albans, Vermont, by Confederates
based in Canada certainly did not help the situation. Nor
did the raids across the border to the north threatened by
Fenians who somehow hoped to free Ireland from British
domination by attacking British North America. In June
1866 the Fenians finally struck, capturing Fort Erie in
Canada West and defeating the Canadian militia, only
to be repulsed later by British regulars. But the worst
blow came when the American Congress, more for pro-
tectionist reasons than to embarrass British North America, decided to end the Reciprocal Trade Treaty. This
effectively killed the hopes of those in New Brunswick
who were looking for increased prosperity based on a

railroad from that colony into Maine and of those in Nova Scotia who had hoped for a great increase in sea-going trade with New England and the mid-Atlantic states.

The dream was not only revived but given increased support by the British government, which saw federation as a way to reduce its huge defense expenditures in British North America. London used its influence on the descendants of the Loyalists in New Brunswick and on the merchants and pro-British citizens of Nova Scotia. Delegates from the two Canadas, Nova Scotia, and New Brunswick convened in London in November 1866. The leading figure was John A. Macdonald, zealous in support of federation. Agreement did not take long and the British North America Act was given Royal Assent on March 29, 1867, to take effect on July 1. Thus was born the Dominion of Canada, something less than a nation, something more than a colony. It is that date that was celebrated in Montreal with Expo 67.

Although this new dominion shared the continent with the United States, it owed its political heritage more to Great Britain. There were two great differences with its southern neighbor. Canada believed, with Britain, in a sovereign Parliament; consequently, its executive power was vested in a Cabinet with its prime minister chosen by the ruling party in the House of Commons. Further, the Canadians were deeply suspicious of the principle of states' rights which they saw as a cause

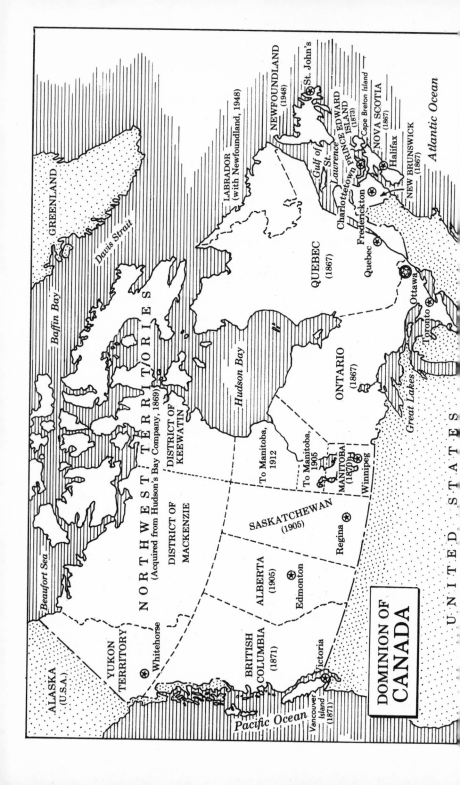

DOMINION OF
CANADA

ALASKA
(U.S.A.)

YUKON
TERRITORY

Whitehorse

BRITISH
COLUMBIA
(1871)

Victoria

Vancouver
Island
(1871)

Pacific Ocean

Beaufort Sea

N O R T H W E S T   T E R R I T O R I E S
(Acquired from Hudson's Bay Company, 1869)

DISTRICT OF
MACKENZIE

ALBERTA
(1905)

Edmonton

SASKATCHEWAN
(1905)

Regina

Baffin Bay

Davis Strait

GREENLAND

DISTRICT OF
KEEWATIN

Hudson Bay

To Manitoba,
1912

To Manitoba,
1905

MANITOBA
(1870)

Winnipeg

ONTARIO
(1867)

Toronto

Ottawa

Great Lakes

LABRADOR
(with Newfoundland, 1948)

NEWFOUNDLAND
(1948)

St. John's

QUEBEC
(1867)

Quebec

*Gulf of
St.
Lawrence*

Charlottetown

PRINCE EDWARD
ISLAND
(1873)

Fredericton

NEW BRUNSWICK
(1867)

Cape Breton Island

NOVA SCOTIA
(1867)

Halifax

Atlantic Ocean

U N I T E D   S T A T E S

of the great American Civil War. They wanted a strong central government with any powers unspecified reverting to the central government rather than the provinces. Ironically, in view of what was to happen later, everyone in Canada, both opponents and supporters, assumed that the provinces would have a minor and subordinate role, with their powers little changed from those they held as colonies. The provinces were to have limited powers of taxation and were authorized to legislate only on matters of local interest. Macdonald put it this way:

> We have strengthened the General Government. We have given the General Legislature all the great subjects of legislation. We have conferred on them, not only specifically and in detail, all the powers which are incident to sovereignty, but we have expressly declared that all subjects of general interest not distinctly and exclusively conferred upon the local governments and local legislatures, shall be conferred upon the General Government and Legislature. . . . This is precisely the provision which is wanting in the Constitution of the United States. It is here that we find the weakness of the American system—the point where the American Constitution breaks down. It is in itself a wise and necessary provision. We thereby strengthen the Central Parliament and make the Confederation one people and one government, instead of five peoples and five governments, with merely a point of authority connecting us to a limited and insufficient extent.[4]

This is the great irony in Canadian history. The founders of a unified Canadian nation were fearful that the principle of states' rights could lead to disintegration.

Yet in the United States the historic trend since the Civil War has been away from states' right to an increase in the powers of the federal government, while in Canada, as we shall soon see, the very thing that its founders sought to prevent—the possession of significant powers by the provinces—would come to pass.

But that was still some years off. For the moment the federationists had every reason to be pleased. The four provinces: Quebec (the former Lower Canada and Canada East), Ontario (the former Upper Canada and Canada West), Nova Scotia, and New Brunswick were soon to be joined by others. Manitoba joined in 1870; British Columbia (upon being promised a transcontinental railroad) joined in 1871; and the stubborn Prince Edward Island in 1873. This, plus the purchase of the Northwest from the Hudson's Bay Company in 1869, the cession by Britain of the Arctic Archipelago in 1880, and provincial status for Alberta and Saskatchewan in 1905, completed the dream of one dominion from sea to sea. Almost. The hardy Newfoundlanders kept their faces turned to the sea until long after the death of the dominion's founding fathers, remaining a separate colony until 1949. It was in 1949, also, that Canada dropped "Dominion," with its implication of subordination, from its name, and became simply Canada.

6

The Growth of Canada

THAT DAY IN 1867 when the Dominion of Canada saw birth was historic, to be sure, but the changes wrought were not magical. The British North America Act had given Canada no new powers and it hardly ensured the survival of the dominion. Indeed, one of its purposes was to enable Britain to withdraw its troops, at a time when Canada had good reason to be wary of its southern neighbor. Overcome for a while by the titanic struggle of the Civil War, American "Manifest Destiny" was once again in full cry. Indeed, it was approaching its most vigorous period, the final decades of the nineteenth century. In the summer of 1867, W.H. Seward, who had purchased Canada's western extension, Alaska, from Russia, declared nothing less than that Nature itself had intended that all of North America come "within the magic circle of the American Union."[1] Even President Andrew Johnson not only defended the acquisition of Alaska as a measure for

". . . extending national jurisdiction and republican principles in the American hemisphere" but he also supported the "acquisition and incorporation into our Federal Union of the several adjacent continental and insular communities as speedily as can be done peacefully, lawfully and without any violation of natural justice, faith or honor. Foreign possession or control of those communities has hitherto hindered the growth and impaired the influence of the United States."[2]

All this, not unsurprisingly, alarmed Canadian leaders and explains the haste with which Macdonald, the first prime minister, acted to solidify the transcontinental nature of the new nation-colony. And Washington, once it saw that Britain was not about to surrender Canada, decided to accept its existence, although many American statesmen assumed that Canada, sooner or later, would fall peacefully into the lap of the United States. Even so a good case can be made for the statement that the United States preserved Canada as a nation. As we saw earlier, Congress, soon after the Civil War, ended the Reciprocal Trade Treaty. This erected a high tariff wall against trade between British North America and the United States. If this wall had not been erected, there would certainly have been increased north-south trade. This, coming in the years when the fragile Dominion of Canada was being constructed, would have made it harder for the advocates of federation to gain supporters. Even after federation, such north-south trade would have weakened the efforts of the central government at Ottawa to tie the new nation-colony together along the east-west axis that existed more in wishful thought than in fact. The widely separated settlements, without any railroad to tie them together, found it easier to trade with Americans just south of the border than among themselves. And American immigrants continued to flood into the wide-open spaces of the Canadian Northwest. It was for this reason that the Canadian leaders poured so much government money into the east-west railroads and for this reason that the Northwest Mounted Police was established. The famous "Mounties" not only ended the Indian wars; they also ensured that American settlers would recognize that they lived under Canadian law. Canada had, no doubt, learned from the melancholy example of Mexico, which had invited American settlers into the vast region of Texas. When the settlers found no effective Mexican law in Texas, they established American law. From then on it had become inevitable that Texas would eventually become annexed to the United States.

The railroad, the famous Canadian Pacific Railway, was the key to Canadian unity. Although there were good economic and physical reasons for having at least some of it dip below the American border, connecting with the great city of Chicago, Macdonald was determined that it be entirely a Canadian railroad. The difficulties were enormous. Not only were the distances immense but the terrain was formidable: mountains, rocky plains, and bottomless marshes. Its construction was halted for years at a time as it got involved with politics. One scandal, although it did not involve him personally, put Macdonald out of power for five years, because railway financiers gave large sums of money to his Conservative party. Although the railroads were supposed to be built with private capital, as they were in the United States, they often ran out of money. The promoters tried desperately to raise additional funds in England, in other parts of Europe, and in the United States. Eventually only the federal government, with its taxing power, could raise the necessary money, and the final spike was not driven until 1885, way behind schedule. The Canadian Pacific became the country's greatest corporation, providing, in addition to rail service, freighters on the Great Lakes and in trade with Europe and the Orient, hotels, roads, and, later, air service. But most of all it opened up the West, taking immigrants to its vast spaces and bringing out its agricultural and mineral riches.

Yet even while Macdonald was viewing with satisfaction his historic successes, the specter that he thought he had put to rest forever arose to haunt him and threaten, not for the first time nor the last, possible disintegration of the fragile federation he had constructed at such great cost. The provinces in the mid-1880s challenged the authority of the federal government. The causes were a complicated mixture of economic and ethnic. A deep depression had set in about 1883, affecting all parts of the country but especially the Maritime Provinces. The steamboat was rapidly replacing the wooden sailing vessels, the construction and operation of which had been crucial to the Maritime economy. This, coinciding with depression, sent thousands of Maritime citizens south to the United States in search of a better life. They were joined by French-Canadians and others from farther west. The causes of the depression were worldwide but it was easier, and more satisfying, to blame the central government in Ottawa. In Manitoba the Canadian Pacific Railway had been welcomed, but its monopoly position allowed it to charge high rates and when the provincial legislature tried to charter railroads to the south to join the American railroads, the Dominion government promptly disallowed the statutes. The feeling that the farmers were being exploited by the Canadian Pacific was common throughout the western prairies.

The biggest trouble was brewing to the north, where the French-speaking Métis (a people of mixed French and Indian blood) had settled in the wild land of the Saskatchewan valley after an abortive rebellion in Manitoba in 1870. Before confederation the Métis had been the most politically conscious settlers of Manitoba. They were determined opponents of confederation, fearing that their distinctive, semi-primitive way of life would be threatened by English-speaking immigrants. With the coming of confederation, the Métis seized control of the colony and, in 1869, presented the federal government with a series of demands. The following year Ottawa sent one of the last contingents of British soldiers to the region for a show of force, but in general, the government conceded to the demands of the Métis, led by the wily but violent Louis Riel.

By the 1870 Act of Manitoba French and English were to have equal status as languages, and Protestants and Roman Catholics were to have separate schools. Nonetheless, the fears of the Métis were realized. Even though their rights were preserved by law, the law could not preserve their way of life. English-speaking farmers tamed the region, forcing out the Métis, who moved to an area where they could continue their wilder life, trapping beaver and hunting buffalo.

In March of 1885 the situation erupted into a second rebellion. Just what their grievances were this second time is not clear, for the Dominion government seemed determined to do its best to help them. Perhaps it was just a reemergence of their old suspicions. Whatever the reason, the Métis called their old leader, Louis Riel, back to Canada. Riel and his Métis drove out a detachment of Mounties at Duck Lake and his Indian allies ravaged the valley of the North Saskatchewan. Canadian soldiers, nearly eight thousand of them, arrived quickly on the new railroad and swiftly put down the rebellion, capturing Riel in the process. His defense attorney tried to get him to agree to a plea of insanity but he contemptuously refused. The court agreed that he was responsible for his actions and he was condemned to death by hanging.

All during this period Ontario, the seat of the national capital, had been actively advocating provincial rights. Despite the depression, Ontario was becoming increasingly industrialized and urbanized and it wanted a greater voice in its own development. It did not want to see the profits from its resources being used to shore up other sections of the country, which was, we must remember, still less than twenty years old, a short time for a national consciousness to grow in a people spread so thinly over so enormous an area.

Quebec until then had been the calmest of all the provinces. With its conservative, authoritarian, clergy-dominated society, it had gone along with Macdonald, who had always been careful to do nothing to arouse it. But suddenly Quebec became enraged. Louis Riel became an instant martyr, however unlikely a choice for that role. The depth of his religious conviction was dubious, he was of mixed blood, and he was a rebel. But his name and his tongue were French and that was enough to arouse the ancient antagonisms. The French-Canadians saw him as a brave defender of French culture against the hated English Protestants. In Ontario the people clamored for his execution and in Quebec they pleaded for the life of this misguided patriot. For a while the French pleas gained reprieves for Riel but finally, on November 16, 1885, he was hanged.

Within a year Honoré Mercier led a nationalist movement, which won an election and formed a government that was a vigorous champion of French-Canadian rights. This in turn enraged those English-Canadians who had long believed that the only true Canadian spoke English and was loyal to the British crown. This backlash, to use a current term, caused the Manitoba legislature to overturn the guarantees written in the Manitoba Act of 1870. The legislature abolished denominational schools, which was seen by Roman Catholics in the province and by French-Canadians in Quebec to be the very thing they had been concerned about from the beginning: the submergence of the French culture.

At this moment of terrific strain, Macdonald, like the French, saw happening just what he feared most. The provinces had taken their challenges of the federal system to the British courts and, to Macdonald's horror, these courts interpreted the British North America Act according to the very precedents, those of the United

States, that Macdonald had been at such great and explicit pains to repudiate. These interpretations, which seemed curious in view of the clear intent of the founders of the Dominion, greatly strengthened the provinces. In 1887 Mercier, although at odds with the other provinces over French-Canadian *survivance*, invited them to join him in a conference to discuss federal-provincial relations. Only British Columbia and Prince Edward Island declined. The conference did not have any real powers; nevertheless, it was a sign that the fragile confederation was in trouble, trouble compounded by the country's severe economic difficulties. During these difficult times there was an active interest in some closer association with the United States. Some advocated a "commercial union," in which the United States and Canada would have no trade restrictions between them and have a joint tariff barrier against the rest of the world. There were even those who advocated annexation, foremost among them Goldwin Smith, a former professor at Oxford and Cornell who had moved to Toronto. He argued that confederation had failed, that there was no national consciousness, that there were compelling economic reasons for annexation and, furthermore, that Canada was not strong enough in itself to assimilate the French-Canadians whom he, like many English-Canadians, saw as backward and priest-ridden.

In spite of everything, Canada somehow stayed together as Prime Minister Macdonald used the tactic that gave him his nickname, Old Tomorrow. Problems he could not solve, he simply ignored, postponing decisions until the passage of time had drained them of their urgency. Perhaps this was not a textbook method of government but in the chaos of Canada in the 1880s it seemed to work. He also, with his enormous prestige and unequaled knowledge of his country and countrymen, appealed to some deeper national instinct, one beyond material gain. He found, as he knew he would, a loyalty even stronger than the real and powerful divisive forces. Now seventy-five, he threw himself into his final election campaign, that of 1891. He argued that the Liberal program of unrestricted trade reciprocity with the United States — although there was far from any guarantee that the United States would have agreed to such a policy — would have made annexation inevitable.

> The question which you will shortly be called upon to determine resolves itself into this: Shall we endanger our possession of the great heritage bequeathed to us by our fathers, and submit ourselves to direct taxation for the privilege of having our tariff fixed at Washington, with the prospect of becoming ultimately a portion of the American Union? . . . As for myself, my course is clear. A British subject I was born — a British subject I will die. With my utmost effort, with my latest breath, will I oppose the "veiled treason" which attempts by sordid means and mercenary proffers to lure our people from their allegiance.[3]

The election came on March 6, 1891. One day early

in May something happened to Macdonald's speech. On May 29 came the final stroke and for eight days he lay silent, until his death. An anxious nation and Empire waited for the end. When it came, Canada had lost its greatest citizen. He had won his last battle: to defeat "continentalism." But the issue would rise again and again. It exists today and some bitter Canadians define continentalism this way: What is in the United States is American. What is in Canada belongs to the entire continent; that is to say, to America.

Macdonald won his last election campaign but within a few years his party would lose something else to which he had dedicated his political life: a strong central government. As always in Canada, three crucial issues were intermixed. We have seen how Macdonald in his last battle won a temporary victory over continentalism. But his party would lose in a bitter dispute that involved the other two issues: province versus federal, French versus English. It is necessary to backtrack slightly. As we saw, the execution of Louis Riel, the Métis leader, had brought to power in Quebec the French-Canadian nationalist Honoré Mercier. He was looking for a bold stroke to strengthen his cause. He found it and set off a chain of related explosions. The Jesuits, who had been expelled from Canada in the 1770s as a result of an intra-Church fight, had returned as a teaching order in the 1840s. They were vigorously anti-Liberal, but Mercier saw a way to undercut their opposition and dramatize the French-Canadian cause. In 1888 he rammed through the Quebec legislature a bill that gave the Church a large financial compensation for the Jesuits' estates that had been confiscated by the English more than a century before at the time of the Conquest. This raised a terrible storm in English Ontario and indirectly stimulated agitation in Manitoba to end the public-supported Roman Catholic schools. In 1890 the Manitoba legislature established a completely non-sectarian school system.

The Roman Catholics in Manitoba, and elsewhere, believed that their guaranteed rights had been violated. The Catholics eventually appealed to the government which, being Conservative, believed in a strong federal government and weak provinces. After considerable hesitation the federal government instructed Manitoba to amend its school legislation in favor of the Catholics. Manitoba refused and the Conservative government did not know what to do. Since it was the party of both the dominant English Protestants and the conservative French-Canadians, it was split at its highest levels. The French-Canadian Cabinet ministers and the Roman Catholic hierarchy insisted upon remedial federal legislation. The Protestant Conservatives were just as adamantly opposed. After a terribly divisive internal conflict, the government decided upon remedial legislation, but before it could be forced through a restive Parliament, the government's term of office ran out.

The election of 1896 was fought on the issue of provincial rights versus federal authority. Macdonald's Conservative party was torn asunder. The English Protestants all over the country voted for the Liberals and, strangely enough, so did French Quebec. On the surface this did not seem to make sense. Why would the French-Canadians vote against the Roman Catholic hierarchy? But the contradiction was more apparent than real. There was, to be sure, a certain amount of anti-clericalism, but a better explanation is to be found in the fact that Mercier's Liberal party in Quebec had become the party of French-Canadian nationalism and the leading figure of the national Liberal party was Wilfred Laurier, who, with his party's victory, became prime minister for fifteen consecutive years, the longest such tenure in Canadian history.

Even more destructive of Macdonald's dream of a strong central government was the Judicial Committee of the Privy Council in London, the supreme court of appeal for the entire Empire. At the beginning the Committee generally accepted the Macdonald interpretation of the British North America Act of 1867. For good reason, since the Act in the most specific language possible had reserved any unspecified rights to the federal legislature. But then in the 1890s the Committee came under the influence of one of its members, Lord Watson, who, for reasons not yet understood, turned the British North America Act topsy-turvy, greatly strengthening the powers of the provinces.

Thus the nineteenth century came to an end. It had been dominated by Macdonald, whose great, historic triumph was his presiding over the founding of Canada and holding it together in its first, fragile decades. But his victories were only temporary and the same battles would have to be fought over and over again in the twentieth century.

7

The New Century

In one of those cycles that perplex economists, the new century brought with it prosperity and for a while Canada's problems were submerged in the rapid, almost fantastic growth of the nation-colony. There was good land in the Northwest and plenty of it. Canada advertised all over the world for immigrants and they came in great numbers, from the Continent, from the British Isles, and, far from least, from the United States. In 1896 only 16,835 immigrants had come to Canada, but by 1901 there were 55,747 and by 1906, 211,653.[1] They filled up the prairies and soon the great wheat harvests began. Saskatchewan and Alberta were admitted as provinces in 1905 and the boundaries of Manitoba were extended. Wheat filled the barns, railroad cars, warehouses, and ships of Canada and was sent in ever-increasing quantities abroad, particularly to Britain. Although the Liberal party had dropped its historic program of low- or no-tariff trade with the United States and sales were increasing with Britain while decreasing with the United States, the United States began to play an even greater economic role in Canada. American money and American management and technical skills began to pour into Canada while Canada increased its purchases of American goods. And, although they were overshadowed by the agricultural development of the prairies, the mining industries, the important pulp-and-paper industries, and the great hydro-electric plants of Ontario and Quebec started to operate.

The internal problems that had so preoccupied Macdonald seemed to be solving themselves under Laurier, soon to become Sir Wilfred. But this was just a happy illusion and the old strains reappeared, revived not so much by internal developments as by the fact that a stronger Canada was beginning to seek its place in world affairs. The first occasion was the Boer War of 1899 with Britain fighting in South Africa. This was one of those sporadic periods when Britain was proud of its Empire and believed all its peoples should pull together for the common, that is to say, British good. Britain appealed to Canada to send an official contingent. There was a great deal of support for such a move on the part of English-Canadians, who had a great emotional tie to the concept of Empire, but the French-Canadians saw it differently. They felt no particular tie to the British Empire and saw no reason why French-Canadian boys should die in Africa in a cause that meant nothing to them. Sir Wilfred, of course, was a French-Canadian himself but in the face of the rising clamor from English-Canadians, he decided that Canada must participate. Some 7,300 Canadians went off to fight. Volunteers. But even this typical Laurier compromise was far from satisfactory. To the staunch English loyalists such token participation meant letting down the Empire, while many French-Canadians saw it as a precedent for deeper involvement in the future. Indeed, it was a foreshadowing of the great conscription crisis of World War I.

The next venture into foreign affairs concerned not the French-English conflict but Canadian-American relations. This time the problem was a boundary dispute, not along the frontier separating the two nations proper but along the Alaskan-Canadian border. An Anglo-Russian Treaty of 1825 had established the border which allowed a narrow strip of Alaska to run down the Pacific shore of northern British Columbia. This became the American-Canadian border when the United States purchased Alaska in 1867. No one paid much attention to such a remote frontier until gold was discovered in the Yukon in 1898. Then Canada decided that the bounda-

ries were not properly drawn and improperly excluded
Canada from access to the sea. Even Canadian historians concede that Canada did not have a good case but
Canadian statesmen of that time thought otherwise.
Canada raised the question and the new President of the
United States, Theodore Roosevelt, made it clear that he
believed the Canadian claim preposterous. In March
1902 he sent troops to southern Alaska, conforming to
the second part, if not the first, of his frequently expressed maxim: "Speak softly and carry a big stick." He
was fully prepared to use force "To run the line as we
claim it, by our own people."[2] He preferred, however, a
peaceful settlement—of his own choosing. He turned
down Canadian proposals to send the matter either to
the Hague Court or to arbitration with a neutral outsider
as umpire. Roosevelt insisted on a judicial judgment,
apparently totally certain of the strength of the American case. The Canadians wanted to avoid military conflict, no doubt influenced by Roosevelt's careless remark
that such trouble "would be death for them."

In January 1903 the two governments agreed that the
boundary would be determined by a tribunal of "six
impartial jurists of repute who shall consider judicially
the questions submitted to them, each of whom shall
first subscribe an oath that he will impartially consider
the arguments and evidence presented to the tribunal and
will decide thereupon according to his true judgement."
Each side would nominate three jurists.

The U.S. Senate was even less disposed than Roosevelt to make any concessions and it didn't like all that talk of impartiality. After all, to obtain a majority decision, at least one panelist would have to vote against his own country. The Senate wanted to make sure that panelist was not an American. Roosevelt avoided any possibility of the Senate's refusing to ratify the agreement by letting that body know who his nominees would be: Elihu Root, the Secretary of War who had sent the troops to Alaska; Senator George Turner of Washington, whose violent opposition to concessions was well known; and Senator Henry Cabot Lodge of Massachusetts, who had publicly condemned the Canadian case. So much for American impartiality.

Needless to say, quite a furor arose in Canada when Roosevelt's appointments were announced. But all would not be lost if the British side was as "impartial" as the American. However, despite the increasing measure of Canadian home rule, foreign affairs still were in the hands of Britain. Britain appointed to the panel two Canadians, one English-speaking, the other French and, as the third member, Lord Alverstone, Lord Chief Justice of England. No Canadian was surprised when Lord Alverstone voted with the Americans. It's entirely possible that he genuinely agreed that Canada had no case. On the other hand, the United States was taking no chances and put great diplomatic pressure on Britain to ensure a satisfactory outcome. As Teddy Roosevelt put it in his characteristically straightforward way, London "tipped the wink to the Chief Justice."

Canadian historian Donald Creighton wrote that the United States undoubtedly had a strong legal case, but he pointed out that the long series of circumstances that preceded the award, and the record of "brutal imperialism" on both sides of the Atlantic had produced in Canada a nationalist reaction "more violent and sustained" than any in the nation's history. The Canadians simply believed that they were the victims of American and British imperialism.[3]

The Alverstone affair made several things clear. First, Canada would sooner or later have to take a more active part in foreign affairs, rather than leave things up to London. Second, so many matters were of joint Canadian-American concern that there would have to be some arrangement for handling them. Both these problems were dealt with in 1909, with the establishment of a Canadian Department of External Affairs (although the final say still rested with London) and an International Joint Commission with three American and three Canadian members. Given a suitable technical staff, it was first empowered to deal with questions concerning bodies of water that crossed or straddled the international boundary. It was also empowered to act as a tribunal of arbitration on any matters referred to it by agreement of both sides. Since the day of its establishment the I.J.C. has done an enormous amount of useful work in arbitrating matters, largely technical in nature, about which differences have arisen.

Sir Wilfred Laurier's differences with his own French-

Canadian people, which flared briefly at the time of the Boer War in 1899, had largely disappeared, for they were enormously proud of him, but these differences were to emerge again ten years later and again over the same issue: Canadian participation in defense of the Empire. In 1909 Britain became alarmed over the increased naval construction of Germany and she appealed to the colonies for help. She would have preferred that Canada contribute money for the augmentation of the British fleet, liking to believe that there should be one Empire, one fleet. But Canada had long been wary of being swallowed up by the Empire. Take pride in it, cooperate with it, but be careful not to be swallowed up by it. Consequently, Sir Wilfred proposed that Canada develop its own small navy of cruisers and destroyers which could, if Parliament so authorized, be put under the command of the British Admiralty in time of imperial emergency.

Again Sir Wilfred tried to find a compromise that could be accepted by both the English- and French-speaking communities. Again the proposal came under fire from both sides. The English imperialists thought it absurd that Canada should have its own navy. Canada should help strengthen the British navy. The French community, on the other hand, as it had a decade before, saw no reason for Canada to get involved in Britain's quarrels an ocean away. This time the French-Canadian opposition was more serious because it had a brilliant leader, Henri Bourassa. He was a man of genuine intellectual stature, an eloquent speaker, and a descendant of the legendary Louis Joseph Papineau. He argued that Laurier's proposal would, to use Laurier's own words, drag Canada into "the vortex of European militarism." The next step, argued Bourassa, would be the conscription of French-Canadian youths to fight in wars that were of no concern to Canada.

Laurier's Naval Bill passed in 1910 but the political storm did not pass with it. Suddenly, however, Laurier saw a chance to divert the nation's attention from this divisive controversy and still again we see how the basic issues intertwine. After years of American disinterest in a reciprocal tariff agreement, President William Howard Taft found himself in political trouble at home because of tariff problems and he suggested to Canada that the two nations agree to free trade in natural and some manufactured products. Laurier simply assumed that most Canadians would welcome such an agreement, particularly since it came as an American offer and not as the result of one of those humiliating Canadian pilgrimages to Washington.

Washington and Ottawa quickly reached agreement and Taft got Congressional approval in the summer of 1911. Now it was up to the Canadian Parliament. At first the Conservative opposition was reluctant to attack the proposal. The manufacturers who favored high tariffs were naturally against it, but they supported the Conservatives anyway and Laurier had beaten them in four consecutive elections. To Laurier's astonishment, opposition began to appear, however, within his own party as well as the Conservative. Rather than try to force it through Parliament, Laurier decided to call for a national election, confident that the voters would support him.

Laurier was wrong. The opposition was not economic, it was emotional. Canadian suspicion of the United States, never very far below the surface, quickly emerged. There was the Alverstone affair of eight years ago. More important there was the imperial "big stick" foreign policy of the United States in the Caribbean and the Pacific.[4] Laurier found himself on the defensive from the beginning. The opposition seldom discussed the tariff agreement in economic terms but rather as the first step toward American annexation of Canada. The opponents took the statements of responsible American political figures out of context but other American politicians made statements more imperialistic than any Conservative propagandist would have dared compose. J. Beauchamp (Champ) Clark, the Democrat who had been designated as Speaker of the next House of Representatives, declared that he was for the reciprocal trade agreement

. . . because I hope to see the day when the American flag will float over every square foot of the British North American posessions clear to the North Pole. . . . I have no doubt whatever that the day is not far distant when Great Britain will joyfully see all her North American possessions become part of this Republic. That is the way things are tending now.[5]

No disclaimers from Washington could stop Canadian newspapers and politicians from seizing on such statements with glee. On the eve of election, the Conservative leader, Robert L. Borden, declared that "We must decide whether a spirit of Canadianism or of Continentalism is to prevail on the northern half of this continent."[6] By the time they went to the polls, many proclaiming the slogan, "No truck nor trade with the Yankees," a majority seemed to agree with Rudyard Kipling. The celebrated English poet had intervened in the campaign with these dramatic words:

> It is her own soul that Canada risks today. Once that soul is pawned for any consideration Canada must inevitably conform to the commercial, legal, financial, social and ethical standards which will be imposed upon her by the sheer admitted weight of the United States.[7]

Thus opposed by the emotional Canadian nationalism in English-speaking Canada and the emotional French-Canadian nationalism of Quebec, poor Sir Wilfred didn't have a chance. He, like Macdonald, had dedicated his political life to the preservation and strengthening of the Canadian federation. He, like Macdonald, had won some important battles, but no final victories. The three great questions remained. And the further advance of Canada onto the world stage would increase the strains.

8

Full Independence

ROBERT L. BORDEN had defeated Laurier and his victory meant that he had inherited Laurier's problems. As World War I drew closer, there was increased pressure on Canada to help the British navy. Although Borden, like Laurier, was a Canadian nationalist, as a member of the English community there was even greater pressure on him. He decided then to do what Britain preferred: not build a small Canadian navy as Laurier had proposed but contribute enough cash to build three battleships. The Liberals in Parliament fought this proposal

fiercely, joined by some Quebeckers who had supported
Borden in the 1911 election. Only by a rigorous application of party discipline did the measure pass the House
of Commons. It was blocked, however, in the Liberal-
controlled Senate in the most important clash between
the two bodies in Canadian history. Consequently, when
war broke out in Europe in 1914, Canada had adopted
neither Laurier's nor Borden's naval policy.

World War I brought a great change to Canada, as it
did to the United States. It caused both North American
nations to venture into the outside world, a venture that
pleased neither of them and resulted in their shrinking
back later into temporary and futile isolation. Though
the United States tried to stay out of the war, Canada
was in it from the first moment. Canada, it must be remembered, although self-governing, was still a colony.
It was legally at war from the beginning, but as it had
long made clear, Ottawa, and not London, would determine the extent of Canadian participation in any way
involving the Empire. Immediately Canada made it
plain that it would participate in a major way. The reason was well expressed by the Canadian historian Gerald M. Craig:

> They rejoiced in the name of Canadians and adamantly
> opposed any tendencies toward "Downing Street rule";
> but, solely as Canadians, they were a small and insignifi-
> cant people. As British subjects, however, they were full
> and equal members in what they firmly believed to be

the grandest political community the world had ever known — one that was a force for good around the globe. Membership in this community, for all the occasional irritations, had made it possible for Canadians to build the Dominion of which they were so proud; a deep sense of loyalty, felt equally by the far-off Australians and New Zealanders, made response almost instinctive when the center of this civilization was in danger. Response would never again be quite so spontaneous, but neither would Canadians ever again be quite so sure of their place in the world's scheme as they were in 1914. The current search for a "Canadian identity" would have made little sense to men of 1914.[1]

That was no doubt true though Craig would have done better to specify English-Canadians, for the response from French-Canadians was by no means so wide or so deep. This division, ancient but active, was to have terrible consequences, as we shall soon see.

Canadian troops were in the thick of the fighting from the first months of 1915 and they suffered appalling, sickening casualties as the incompetent French and British generals poured wave after wave of human cannon fodder toward the German trenches. So terrible were the casualties that Canada, with one-tenth the population of the United States, suffered about the same number of killed and wounded. That was why, when finally the awful war was over, it often griped Canadians to hear Americans claim that they had won the war, however true it might be that the entrance of American doughboys tilted the balance. For the Canadians knew that their contribution had been great. As Lloyd George wrote in his war memoirs:

> The Canadians played a part of such distinction [on the Somme in 1916] that thenceforward they were marked out as storm troops; for the remainder of the war they were brought along to head the assault in one great battle after another. Whenever the Germans found the Canadian Corps coming into the line they prepared for the worst.[2]

The size of the Canadian war effort made it more a powerful ally than just a colony. By 1917 between a quarter and a third of the shells fired by the British armies were manufactured in Canada. It also produced high explosives, rifles, ships, and airplanes. The vast wheatfields of central and western Canada helped feed the Empire. The war caused expansion in the newsprint industry and in the mining of copper, nickel, and lead, and the preoccupation of British industry with the war effort caused Canadian manufacturers to gain a larger share of the domestic market. Canada was fully conscious of its greater importance, as evidenced in a letter from Prime Minister Borden to the Canadian high commissioner in London:

> It can hardly be expected that we shall put 400,000 or 500,000 men in the field and willingly accept the position of having no more voice and receiving no more consideration than if we were toy automata. Any person cherishing such an expectation harbours an unfortunate

and even dangerous delusion. Is this war being waged by the United Kingdom alone, or is it a war waged by the whole Empire?[3]

When Lloyd George became the British prime minister toward the end of 1916, he immediately changed his nation's policy, inviting the prime ministers of the dominions to become members of the Imperial War Cabinet. By the following year the Canadian Corps was at its height. In 1917 it won a series of brilliant victories but they took a terrible toll. By the spring of 1917, Prime Minister Borden, who had spent months in London, was convinced that conscription, a draft, was necessary. Nearly four hundred thousand Canadians had enlisted, an extraordinary voluntary effort, equal to about five million in the United States with its population ten or twelve times that of Canada. But Borden was convinced that Canada had to provide a half million men. Since the number of those eager to serve had already been exhausted and industry and agriculture were competing for young men, the only possible way to get them was to draft them.

The draft was to reopen, and make more grievous, old wounds. French Canada had never questioned the legitimacy of Canada's participation in the war. Nor had it questioned the conviction that Canada's participation had to be substantial. Perhaps its definition of "substantial" was different from that of English Canada for what it did question was the enormity of the participation. This is not to suggest that only French-Canadians questioned the draft. Organized labor did and so did farmers but the French opposition was strongest. This, of course, had clearly been foreshadowed by French-Canadian opposition to Canadian participation in the Boer War of 1899 and to helping build up the British navy in the pre-war years.

The French were the first Canadians and their loyalty was to Canada, particularly French Canada. They had been separated from France for a century and a half, and so there was no historic reason for them to be attached to Britain. They supported the allies, to be sure, but without the passion that characterized the support of English Canada. The Canadian army, after all, spoke English; its officers came for the most part from the English community; and it served with British forces. Furthermore, the French suspicions of the English, always, as we have seen, close to the surface, were revived when Ontario, the heart of English Canada, limited the use of French as a language of instruction and subject for study. The French, once again, felt themselves second-class citizens in the country they had founded. Why, many argued, should they be drafted to fight in a remote war when they were not treated like full-fledged citizens at home? The response of English Canada was just the opposite. Many regarded the French-Canadians as shirkers and saw conscription as a way to force them to shoulder their share of the burden.

Once again we see the inability of either side to understand the other, although it seems fair to suggest that over the decades English Canada, as the dominant majority, had not made sufficient efforts to understand the deeply held convictions of the French minority.

In October 1917 Prime Minister Borden formed a coalition government, inviting Liberals to join his Conservatives in the Cabinet. Obviously, he was hoping for a united front on the issue of the draft. But Laurier, although he had vigorously supported the war effort to this point, could not go along on the issue of the draft. Borden called an election for December. With the support of pro-draft Liberals, mainly from the western provinces, joined to his Conservatives, the coalition government won handily. For twenty years it had seemed that national unity was growing but suddenly the government was entirely in the hands of English-Canadians. Quebec, and the other French enclaves, found themselves isolated, and Sir Wilfred Laurier, who had devoted his political life to national unity, was supported only by his own French-Canadians. The bitter feelings engendered by that election were to persist for years.

Regardless of the deep division at home, abroad the Canadian army continued its bright record of victory. In the final months of the war the Canadians served as the spearhead of attacks that brought glorious but costly victories. When the war ended, Canada and the other Dominions had a new but, to non-Empire states at least, perplexing status. They were members of the British delegation to the Versailles peace conference and had their own independent delegations as well.

Sometime during the post-war years Canada attained full independence, but it is hard to say exactly when. It was represented at the peace conference and it became a member of the League of Nations. Yet it was still, nominally at least, a subordinate member of the British Empire. The situation was cleared up somewhat in 1926 when the Imperial Conference approved the Balfour Declaration that defined Britain and the dominions as "autonomous communities within the British Empire equal in status, in no way subordinate to one another in any aspect of their domestic or external affairs, though united by a common allegiance to the Crown and freely associated as members of the British Commonwealth of Nations."[4]

The Balfour Declaration was fine but it did not clear up a whole tangle of legal and constitutional ties to Britain. A committee was appointed to deal with these matters and its recommendations were embodied in the 1931 Statute of Westminister which provided that the parliaments of the dominions had full powers of government. But it was not possible to provide a tidy end to the Canadian relationship to the British Parliament. Because of regional and ethnic conflicts, Canada was not able to agree on a method for amending the British North America Acts of 1867 and later years. Since each of the various factions feared that one of the others might seize temporary control of the Canadian government and amend the constitution to its own benefit, Canada insisted on a provision in the Statute of Westminster denying itself the right to amend its own constitution. This could be done only by the British Parliament which would act automatically whenever the Canadian authorities could agree on the changes to ask for. Despite the fact that it has long been evident that Canada's constitution needs amendment, it has not been done to this day because the two cultures, English and French, and the two levels of government, federal and provincial, cannot agree on the distribution of powers.

Meanwhile, Canada was beginning to edge itself cautiously into world affairs. The most important area was its relations with the United States. During the war, for obvious reasons, there had been close liaison between various bodies of the two governments. So involved were the two neighbors by now that at war's end about three-quarters of the work of the British Embassy in Washington was concerned with Canadian matters even though there was little Canadian representation in the embassy. Therefore, Britain and Canada agreed as early as 1920 that Canada should have its own representation in Washington but for some reason this did not occur until 1926, when Canada and the United States established legations. Canada soon established legations also in Paris and Tokyo.

Although Canada was within the League of Nations and the United States was not, Canada was fully as isolationist as its neighbor. In its speeches in Geneva, Canada often referred to the friendly Canadian-American border (a compulsion of government spokesmen on both sides) and suggested that other nations should follow the North American example, without suggesting how that was possible in contentious Europe. Canada, like America, took great solace in the fact that it was so far from Europe. In one 1924 speech the Canadian representative suggested that his country lived "in a fireproof house far from inflammable materials" and hence should not have to pay very high fire insurance premiums.

Clearly Canada was edging closer to the United States and this trend was speeded up under a new prime minister, William Lyon Mackenzie King, a descendant of the earlier reformer whose name he bore. With the end of the war effective coalition government had ended along with the end of prosperity, so Canada was once again in a period of upheaval. There were demonstrations by farmers and workers who, in a bewildered way, felt a sense of injustice aroused by war profiteering at home and by the hopes, however uncertain, raised abroad by the Russian revolution. These grievances led to the birth of farmer and labor parties that attacked not only national policies, but also the old parties which had promoted them.[5]

A new party, the Progressive party, was formed in

1920. It got its strength from western farmers and workers. The old parties sought to meet its challenge by internal reform. The wartime prime minister, Sir Robert Borden, retired as head of the Conservative party in favor of Arthur Meighen and W. L. Mackenzie King succeeded Sir Wilfred Laurier, who had died in 1919, as head of the Liberals. Of the two older parties the Liberals most successfully accommodated themselves to the spirit of reform in the air. Their platform in 1919 was filled with the language of social reform. During 1920 and 1921 the Conservative government lost its wartime vigor and was under constant attack from the Progressives and the Liberals, once again more or less reunited. In December 1921, the Liberals, led by Mackenzie King, won handily, taking 117 seats in the House. The Conservatives fell down badly, winning only 50 seats compared to 65 for the Progressives.

Although King had spoken the language of a reformer, when he took office he turned out to be as conservative as the Conservatives. ". . . he soon revealed a caution so deep-seated and pervasive that a generation of historians and commentators has failed to find adjectives adequate to describe it, despite an enthusiastic search."[6] His natural caution was not all; he also had some political and constitutional difficulties. The Liberal party, although it had a bare majority in the House, was hardly homogeneous. It had two distinct wings. One was more or less genuinely liberal, coming from the West which was also the heart of the Progressive party. But many Liberals were conservative French-Canadians who belonged to the party simply because it was the opposition to the hated Conservatives who had pushed through the draft. Also the old provincial-federal dispute was reasserting itself. During the war the federal government, through necessity, had assumed many of the powers it had possessed originally but which had been given to the provinces by Lord Watson's judicial decisions. For a time it seemed as if the Watson view of the distribution of powers was dead forever, but in the early 1920s the provinces again appealed to the British Judicial Committee of the Privy Council. Its leading light was Viscount Haldane, an uncritical admirer of his predecessor, Lord Watson. He decreed that the federal government could exercise such extended powers only in a wartime emergency. It was thus Haldane who completed the destruction of John Macdonald's dream of a strong central government. His decisions provided Canada with two constitutions — one for use in peace, the other for war. It was a time of peace now, and the central government found itself hemmed in by the power of the provinces in relation to legislation in the fields of property and civil rights.[7]

While King struggled along, usually in power, sometimes out, the Canadian North enjoyed a fantastic boom. With American capital playing the major role, the mining and paper-and-pulp industries grew at a rapid rate, with most of the products going to the United States, thus reestablishing the north-south axis of trade that had alarmed Canadian nationalists in the past and would again. Crucial also was the fact that the development of natural resources lay within the power of the provinces, a power jealously guarded, making it difficult for the federal government to establish a national policy. This, as we shall see, is a major factor in the current controversy over American investment in Canada.

Although it often seems at the time as if an economic boom will last forever, they seldom do. When the bottom fell out of the American economy in the fall of 1929, it was only a matter of months before Canada was affected, for already its economy was closely tied to that of the United States. When the depression began in Canada in 1930, King assumed, like leaders in most countries, that it was just another of those periodic downturns that would soon right itself. Consequently, he made no effort to combat falling prices and rising unemployment. The Conservative leader, Richard B. Bennett, however, promised to take vigorous measures to end the depression and so his party won a resounding victory in the 1930 elections. Some historians have suggested that King's loss was really lucky, for he went out at the very beginning of the depression, leaving poor Bennett to cope with its worst years. When Bennett finally fell victim to the depression, King swept back into power, which the Liberals retained for an extraordinary twenty-two years beginning in 1935. It was very similar to the situation in the United States, where the Democrats, gaining power during the worst of the depression, held onto it for twenty years.

The Canadian depression, like the American, was terrible. The forestry and mining industries suffered from world conditions and suffered even more when in 1930 President Herbert Hoover signed the Smoot-Hawley Tariff, the highest in American history. This made it even more difficult to sell in the United States the products of Canadian mines and forests. The situation was even worse on the prairies. In the first place, the collapse of world prices for wheat and the erection of tariff barriers were both severe blows to the Canadian farmers. Then nature hit the prairies with drought, dust storms, and disease. Not only were prices low but the Canadian farmers had little to sell.

Prime Minister Bennett tried hard to end the depression but he was too conservative and when, in 1935, he tried to imitate the imaginative and drastic steps taken by Franklin D. Roosevelt for the United States, it was too late. Before such measures could take effect, his party's term of office was up and he had to face an election. Mackenzie King triumphed easily and moved into a close relationship with Roosevelt that lasted through the final years of the depression and through the war. Soon after taking office, King asked the Judicial Committee of the Privy Council in London for an advisory opinion on the sweeping measures proposed by Bennett. Again demonstrating its inability, or refusal, to understand the clear language of the British North America Act, the Committee declared almost all the proposals to be beyond the power of the federal government. There was little King could do, although certain trade arrangements with the United States helped some, and Canada, like the United States, was gripped by depression until the outbreak of World War II.

Before turning to that war, with its profound influence on Canada, the United States, and their relationship, we should look briefly at an area that had come to concern Canadians — the American domination of Canadian culture. During the late 20s and the 30s there was an explosion of American popular culture. American movies and American magazines began to appear all over Canada and, most pervasive, American radio stations, for most of Canada's ten millions lived along the border, well within reach of United States broadcasters. American sports heroes — Babe Ruth, Bill Tilden, and Jack Dempsey — became heroes in Canada as well, as did American movie stars and radio personalities. The whole world was influenced by American culture . . .

But Canadians were closest to this vigorous outburst, which poured irresistibly across a truly undefended border. Most of them consumed the new culture as readily, and as expertly, as did Americans, yet inevitably their reactions were somewhat different from their neighbors'.

Even while they were being amused and thrilled—in a restrained Canadian fashion, of course—they indulged themselves in a certain sense of disapproval, like a maiden aunt who was titillated but who felt she ought to be shocked. Many indications of Canadian opinion revealed a strong belief that they were more honest, more moral, more religious than Americans who allowed easy divorce, let gangsters dominate their lives, and tolerated corruption in all phases of their national life. If any of these and countless other deplorable characteristics appeared in Canada, they were merely taken as evidence of insidious American influence.[8]

The author of the above words, himself a Canadian, wrote that such Canadian opinion was omitted or softened from a volume on Canadian-American relations to "prevent a book in a series designed to promote the course of international goodwill from itself being a source of irritation."[9]

It seems true even today, more than thirty years later, that English-Canadians act very much like Americans, although with a bit more restraint. During the 1930s, the Canadian government became sensitive to the possibility of a natural Canadian culture being overwhelmed by that of the United States. It was during these years that the government established the Canadian Broadcasting Corporation, a government-financed but independent radio and (now) television network that has probably done more than any other institution to develop, preserve, and spread a Canadian culture. However, it has been inevitable — because of a common cultural heritage, because of the sheer weight of American culture — that the two nations should have a common culture, except, of course, in French Canada, where the difference in language makes a very real difference indeed. In fact, a very strong case can be made for the argument that any real difference in Canadian and American culture depends almost entirely on the existence of a peculiar French-Canadian culture.

9

World War II and After

In the uneasy decades after World War I, Canada, like the United States, fell into a posture of isolationism. Like the United States, it was disillusioned. It had suffered terrible casualties in the "war to end all wars" but it soon became apparent that another war was possible, perhaps even probable. French-Canadians as well as many English-Canadians did not want to become involved in Europe's agonies. When Mackenzie King returned to power in 1935, he recognized that he had to follow a difficult course. Much of his political support came from isolationists, yet he was certain that if Britain were ever in mortal jeopardy, most English-Canadians would feel no alternative but to rush to its rescue. Therefore, he preferred not to talk about foreign affairs and when he did it was in speeches so long and abstruse that his position was difficult to pin down. Generally he relied on such slogans as "no commitments" and "Parliament will decide," obscuring the fact that Canada would have no real choice but to intervene if Britain were imperiled.

Canada was not very active in the League of Nations but that made her little different from the other members who were ineffectual in combating the aggressions of Japan in China and Italy in Ethiopia. Mackenzie King met with Hitler in 1937 and implied that Canada would come to Britain's aid if need be, although he was convinced — or perhaps he convinced himself — that Hitler would soon be satisfied and there would be no general war. It was easy, therefore, for Mackenzie King to become an enthusiastic supporter of the appeasement policy of British Prime Minister Neville Chamberlain.

During these years Canada moved even closer to the United States, a relationship personified by the friendship between Roosevelt and King, which went back to their days at Harvard. In 1938 complex trade negotiations were carried on among Britain, Canada, and the United States. As a result Canada gave up some of her imperial preference in trade with Britain in return for freer entry into the American market. In August of that year, Roosevelt, in Ontario to receive an honorary degree, declared that "The Dominion of Canada is part of the sisterhood of the British Empire. I give to you assurance that the people of the United States will not stand idly by if domination of Canadian soil is threatened by any other Empire." It is hard to see where any such threat to Canada could come from, but in days of crisis — and war was not very far over the horizon — statesmen often speak more for effect than for any substantial reason.

As the war drew nearer, it became obvious that Canada could not remain isolationist. Canada, by the nature of its being and its history, was inescapably tied to the British Empire and the values it represented. Indeed the modern Commonwealth was a Canadian creation and all its resources, material and moral, had been dedicated to the Commonwealth's free institutions, its liberties, its freedom of the seas, and its international trade.[1]

Here one can suggest that this is an English-Canadian view, for it is doubtful that a French-Canadian would have felt quite that identification with the British Empire. Nonetheless, this was the feeling that dominated Canadian policy. Even though Britain was very likely confident that it could again count on Canada — with its increased strength even more valuable than two decades before — it took no chances. In the early summer of 1939 King George and Queen Elizabeth were sent to Canada to cement the ties. The visit was an enormous success.

When German tanks crashed into Poland, there was no doubt what course Canada would follow. Britain declared war on September 3 but this time the imperial declaration was not binding on the entire Empire. Australia and New Zealand immediately declared war. Eire (Ireland) decided to remain neutral. South Africa declared war three days later and Canada took a week, for Mackenzie King, as he had promised long before, called Parliament into special session. On September 10, with the unanimous consent of the Senate and the almost unanimous support of the House, Canada declared war on Germany. Mindful of the draft riots of World War I, Mackenzie King had earlier solemnly promised the French-Canadians that there would be no conscription should it be necessary to go to Britain's aid. And his loyal French-Canadian lieutenant, Ernest Lapointe, had bluntly warned his people that if they attempted to prevent Canadian aid to Britain there would be civil war.

The war would have profound effects on Canada and the United States and on their relationship, for of all the major participants only they would remain relatively untouched by the cruelties of war. In fact, the economies of both nations prospered, became even more intertwined, and at war's end, Canada, although only a small

country in terms of population, had the strongest
military machine in the world after only the United
States, the Soviet Union, and Great Britain.

But all that was in the future. At the moment Canada
could hardly be expected to look beyond the war into
which it threw all its great energy and abundant resources. Such dedication was possible only if Mackenzie King first solved some political problems at home.
The first challenge came from Quebec. Maurice Duplessis, the provincial premier, called for a provincial election, accusing the federal government of intending to
increase the centralization of powers "by involving the
pretext of war."[2] Duplessis, leader of the *Union Nationale* party, declared that nothing less was at stake than
Quebec's identity against the dangers of "participation,
assimilation, and centralization."[3] King decided to accept
the challenge. He did not want to go to war with a hostile government in power in Quebec. Lapointe and the
other French-Canadian members of the Liberal Cabinet
returned home from the capital and campaigned vigorously. They said that if Duplessis's party won, they
would resign their cabinet posts, leaving French Canada
without representation in the federal government. And
they, and Mackenzie King, repeated over and over their
solemn promise that there would be no draft. The intervention of the federal Liberals succeeded and their provincial colleagues won a great victory. Quebec, for the
moment and under the circumstances, was prepared to
support the war.

Just when King thought he had things in hand, another challenge arose, this time in Ontario. Mitchell Hepburn had unloosed a volley of attacks on King, accusing him of not prosecuting the war energetically enough. It was true that Canada had not yet done much, but it was still early and the war in Europe was in that lethargic stage when not much was happening, so little, in fact, that the term "phony war" had become popular. Nonetheless, Hepburn pushed through the Ontario legislature on January 18, 1940 a resolution of censure because "the Federal Government at Ottawa has made so little effort to prosecute Canada's duty in the war in the vigorous manner the people of Canada desire to see."[4] This was seen by many as a not very subtle rebuke to King for promising the French-Canadians there would be no draft, a measure thought essential by many English-Canadians.

Normally King thought things over a long time before acting but he immediately perceived that Hepburn had given him an opening. The five-year term of his government would be up later that year and elections would have to be held unless he decided as a wartime measure to operate with a coalition government. This he did not want to do. If, however, he held elections later in the year, he would first have to go through a session of Parliament that would enable his critics to attack him in preparation for the election campaign. Perhaps he could use the action of the Ontario legislature as an excuse to call a sudden election. Parliament returned as scheduled

on January 25 for its regular session, members coming
from all across the vast land. No sooner had they assembled than they were given the news that King had decided to go to the voters. The session lasted only an afternoon. Mackenzie King's instinct was right. The voters
flocked to support Liberal candidates and the prime minister ended up with an even bigger majority in the new
House than he had had in the old, the largest majority in
Canadian history up to that time. King wrote in his dia-
ry: "We really cleaned up in the province of Quebec
(every seat but four) and I often thought of what Sir
Wilfred [Laurier] said to me . . . when I told him of my
intention to stand by him . . . against conscription in
(1917) — that I would have the province of Quebec for
the rest of my life."[5] An ironic statement in view of
what would happen later.

King had little time to enjoy his triumph of March
1940 for soon Hitler would unleash the blitzkrieg attacks that would bring the capitulation of Denmark,
Norway, Belgium, Holland, and even mighty France. In
April King took a post-election holiday and spent a few
days with FDR at his favorite resort, Warm Springs,
Georgia. Roosevelt, his hands tied by the Neutrality
Acts passed by Congress a few years before, was trying
to find ways to help the British. And King was becoming convinced that American help was essential.

In May, as German armies raced across a France
which had boasted that it was invulnerable, the terrible
question arose on both sides of the border. Would Brit-

ain be able to hold out? Roosevelt feared that the British navy, then the greatest in the world, might have to be surrendered to spare Britain from conquest. He asked King to persuade Winston Churchill that the navy should not be surrendered under any circumstances. Obviously, FDR did not then know the indomitable Churchill as well as he would later. King sent a message to Churchill saying that if it became necessary for the fleet to leave home waters, the United States would see that it was repaired and refitted in American and Commonwealth ports, would assume the defense of the Atlantic, participate in a tight blockade of Europe and, if Hitler tried to starve Britain into submission, would send food under naval escort, and any interference with the food ships would mean immediate war. Four days later Churchill uttered his imperishable words:

> We shall never surrender, and even if, which I do not for a moment believe, this Island or a large part of it were subjugated and starving, then our Empire beyond the seas, armed and guarded by the British Fleet, would carry on the struggle, until, in God's good time, the New World, with all its power and might, steps forth to the rescue and liberation of the old.[6]

With the fall of France, Britain stood alone in Europe, for the Soviet Union had not yet been invaded by Germany. And with American entrance into the war a year and a half off, the Commonwealth nations, most notably Canada, were Britain's chief hope. Canada poured itself into the rescue mission, so much so that it had few resources left for continental defense. With growing German power, it began to seem that the Atlantic Ocean might not be sufficient defense, especially if valiant Britain should succumb. The United States was alarmed too and on August 17, 1940, Mackenzie King and Roosevelt met at Ogdensburg, New York, on the American side of the St. Lawrence. With only one night for reflection King accepted what was evidently a Roosevelt proposal, that a Permanent Joint Board on Defense be established, with equal membership for the two countries. The cautious King, who had always proclaimed "no commitments," decided on this important step without consulting his colleagues. There was no formal agreement of any kind, just a joint press release of August 18. King's critics wondered why he had so long resisted all proposals for Anglo-Canadian military cooperation when he was willing without reference to Parliament to enter into such a close relationship with the United States. King obviously thought that urgent circumstances required urgent actions.

Later, it was agreed that the United States would assume strategic command of Canadian forces if Britain surrendered or if the Royal Navy lost control of the Atlantic. And even though neither happened, the United States subsequently suggested that it command the forces of both nations. That was further than King was prepared to go. Although he regarded United States-Canadian military cooperation as vital, he did not want Canada slipping into American control. It would be "better to have two peoples and two governments on this continent understanding each other and reciprocating in their relations as an example to the world, than to have anything like continental union."[7] For this same reason Canada declined to participate in the Lend-Lease program that Roosevelt had devised to provide "all aid short of war" to the Allies. However, Canada did require American economic help. It was purchasing such vast quantities of materials from the United States for war use that it ran short of gold and dollars. Roosevelt provided a partial solution by ordering the United States to buy more strategic materials from Canada and by charging Canada's purchases of strategic materials to Britain's Lend-Lease account.

Canada's position as a British ally of the first rank diminished considerably in 1941 with the entrance of the Soviet Union and the United States into the war. Although it contributed mightily in absolute terms and even more in terms of its relative strength, Canada often found itself excluded from the highest councils of war. Conscious of its enormous effort, Canada had every reason to feel neglected. It was merely learning the lesson of world politics: Powerful nations ignore the less powerful unless they need something from them; then the less powerful are expected to do as requested and, if they ask too many questions, the mighty nations become impatient.

Canada, however, did not let hurt feelings stand in the way of doing its duty, in providing both the material and human requirements of modern war. The only threat to this policy could come from internal disunity and no reader will be surprised that it came once again with French-Canadian resentment over conscription. Before the war and in its early months, Mackenzie King and his French-Canadian lieutenants had proclaimed time and time again that Canadians would not be drafted to fight overseas. In mid-1940 the National Resources Mobilization Act gave the government great powers over the economy and also gave it the authority to draft men for home defense. The French-Canadians did not object to that, for they had always been passionate patriots, but for Canada only, not the British Empire. As the war wore on, the question of drafting men for overseas duty inevitably arose and many English-Canadians began to say aloud that their French-speaking compatriots were not bearing their fair share of the burden.

> Back of this insistence, as far as some were concerned, was the view that the war provided an appropriate and highly promising opportunity to require a minority to submit to the will of the majority — more precisely, that French-Canadians would be brought into line and, if necessary, coerced. Such people seemed to feel that, if they could not get at the enemy, at least they could have it out with their fellow Canadians of the other language and religion.[8]

Mackenzie King found himself in a spot. Clearly the majority wanted conscription and just as clearly the French-Canadians, a vital part of his political support, were as opposed as ever. He certainly didn't want the draft riots of World War I all over again. Although Mackenzie King was a cautious man, he did not lack political imagination. He decided to try a novel approach: he would hold a national plebiscite. Without saying whether or not he would impose conscription if permitted to, he asked the voters on April 27, 1942 to answer Yes or No to this question: "Are you in favour of releasing the Government from any obligations arising out of any past commitments restricting methods of raising men for military service?" In Quebec the response was negative: seventy-two percent to twenty-eight, many of the affirmative votes no doubt coming from the sizeable English-speaking minority in Montreal. It would be fair to estimate that the French opposition was about equal in percentage to the English support in the other provinces, eighty to twenty. For the country as a whole the proportion was Yes sixty-four percent and No thirty-six.

Obviously, even though the government had won a substantial majority, the issue was still dangerously divisive. Mackenzie King had to move toward conscription, but he tried to do it in a way that would not further antagonize the French-Canadians. Using a slogan that became famous, "Not necessarily conscription, but conscription if necessary," he pushed through the Parliament a bill removing the limitations on conscription in the National Resources Mobilization Act. Still he made it plain that he would do all he could to avoid using the draft authorization. This brought him attack from both sides. His reluctance to draft men for overseas duty angered the pro-British and the conscription bill angered the French-Canadians. Most of the French-Canadian cabinet ministers protested loudly and the senior one resigned. As the argument dragged out over the summer, King increased the draft calls for the home defense army. This stimulated enlistments for overseas duty in the army and air force of young men who were embarrassed about being drafted for safe, and somewhat disreputable, service in the home defense forces.

The issue simmered for another couple of years as Mackenzie King, to the exasperation of many English-speaking activists, declined to use the draft authority given him. In 1944, however, the Canadian army became involved in heavy and costly fighting on both the northern and southern fronts in Europe. The casualties were terrible and the Minister of Defence, Colonel J. L. Ralston, flew to the fronts to see just how badly reinforcements were needed. He returned convinced that full conscription was necessary, that Mackenzie King must now keep the pledge he had made publicly: to send draftees abroad if necessary.

Mackenzie King summoned the War Committee of the Cabinet on October 19, 1944. Ralston proposed that fifteen thousand soldiers of the home defense force should be sent to Europe immediately. As soon as the

Defence Minister finished, King warned the small elite group that conscription would tear the nation apart in a terrible, irreconcilable conflict. Canada was on the brink of a political crisis of the greatest magnitude.[9] For ten days the War Committee agonized over every possible alternative. King and a majority of the Cabinet, including every member from Quebec, were opposed to conscription. But a strong minority held out, arguing that there was no possible alternative. The frustrating debate could not go on much longer. The nation was finally beginning to get an idea of the deep divisions within the government, and it was uneasy and concerned. The affair threatened to get out of hand and the Prime Minister concluded that the internal conflict could not be permitted to continue. He had to find a solution—if there was one—at once.[10]

Mackenzie King had devoted his political life to the difficult reconciliation of French and English Canada. He had led Canada through a terrible war but now it all seemed to be falling apart. Then at the last possible moment he thought of General A.G. McNaughton, who had retired ten months earlier as commander of the Canadian army when it had been divided and parceled out to various British units. He had had his differences with the High Command in Britain and with civilian and military authority in Canada, but he was widely admired throughout the country as the father of the modern Canadian army. And, most important to King, he had always believed in the principle of voluntary service. King summoned the soldier and asked if he would serve as Minister of Defence, committed publicly to the policy of no draft for overseas service.

McNaughton consented and on November 1, without saying anything to his colleagues, King went to meet with his Cabinet. When Ralston stuck to his position, King astonished his colleagues by announcing that he would accept the resignation Ralston had offered on this issue two years before and appoint McNaughton in his place. The general took office and for three strenuous weeks tried to scare up enough voluntary replacements for the men lost in combat. He could not and Ralston was vindicated. It seemed now that the Mackenzie King government must fall, for whichever position he took — conscription or no conscription — supporters of the other would resign.

Again, and in that time and under those circumstances it was a political drama of compelling force, King pulled off a political miracle. He declared that he would not follow a general policy of sending draftees abroad but in the emergency would send sixteen thousand members of the home defense force to Europe. He was saved by the loyalty of his colleagues, both for and against the draft. The conscriptionists announced that they would remain in the Cabinet and even Ralston, who had been fired, declared that he would support the policy in Parliament. On the other side, Louis St. Laurent, now the most important French-Canadian Cabinet minister, also announced his support. At an absolutely crucial moment, and despite their deep personal convictions, both sides were willing to make a difficult compromise. Perhaps even more important in saving the Mackenzie King government was the fact, now becoming clearer with every day, that the war would soon be over, that the question would not have to arise again. In June 1945, a month after the war ended in Europe, Mackenzie King and his Liberals were returned to power and would lead Canada to closer and closer relations with the United States.

While the election campaign was underway, Mackenzie King was in San Francisco contributing to the birth of the United Nations. This time Canadian participation was in dramatic contrast to its participation in the League of Nations, for since 1945 there has been no more active or loyal supporter of the UN than Canada. Of even greater importance to Canada was its relationship with the United States. During the war it had of necessity increased its trade with the United States and after the war Britain was never able to regain its place in Canadian trade. By 1947 Canada was buying twice as much from the United States as it was selling and this, a problem that has continued to this day, will be discussed in more detail later.

More important for the moment is the increasing intimacy of the military relationship of the United States

and Canada in the immediate postwar years that persisted until well into the 1960s. However, since relationship
implies a certain equality, it might be better to say that
Canada as a conscious policy decided to follow the
American lead, with the United States coming to expect
Canada to follow that lead in every detail. Without
going into the complicated and controversial question of
the origins of the Cold War, subsequent behavior makes
it clear that Canada shared — although not nearly to the
same degree — the American conviction that the Soviet
Union was a threat to the entire "free world." For that
reason Canada shared the United States interest in the
establishment of NATO, the North Atlantic Treaty Or-
ganization. Canada, however, had a further impetus, its
belief that NATO would help in the work Canada had
always seen as its peculiar role, bringing North America
closer to Europe.

It was in bilateral defense relationships that Canada
and the United States were closest. American strategists
were not slow to perceive that any possible attack on the
United States by the Soviet Union would occur by the
shortest route — across the North Pole and across Canada. Although Canadian statesmen were wary about the
effect of American defense installations in Canada, they
had decided to allow such facilities, although nominally
under Canadian sovereignty, in the name of joint defense. The basis of this was made plain on April 29,
1948 in a speech by Louis St. Laurent, who had succeed-

ed to the premiership upon Mackenzie King's retirement: "Our foreign policy . . . must, I suggest, be based on a recognition of the fact that totalitarian communist aggression endangers the freedom and peace of every democratic country, including Canada."[11]

Canada supported the American position when the Korean War broke out in June 1950 with the invasion of South Korea, an American client state, by North Korea, a Russian client state. The invasion followed a series of border incidents and frequent exchanges of accusations between the dictatorial government of South Korean Syngman Rhee and the Communist government of Kim Il Sung. The United States made the unilateral decision to intervene on South Korea's behalf and then decided it would be useful to receive the blessing of the United Nations, which, for its first fifteen years at least, was dominated by the United States and its allies.

The Canadian government accepted the view that the UN had no choice but to fight the North Korean aggressors. There was little sympathy for the view that the UN might be more effective in ending a breach of the peace if it served as a mediator rather than as a participant in the conflict. However, Canada did not share the United States preoccupation with China and when the Chinese Communists won the civil war against Chiang Kaishek's Nationalists in 1949 Canada was prepared to recognize the new Chinese government as soon as it demonstrated its control of the country. Some Canadians were concerned, therefore, when the United States, as soon as the Korean War broke out, sent its Pacific Fleet into position to protect Chiang Kai-shek's forces on Taiwan. This, in effect, involved the United States and the UN in the Chinese civil war. And this was to have adverse effects in Asia and the world for another two decades. Nonetheless, Canada followed the United States lead and did not recognize China.

There was occasionally in those years some fairly mild Canadian criticism of American foreign policy and some testy feeling in the United States that the Canadians would do better to criticize less and concentrate more on pulling their share of the load. It was in this context that Lester B. Pearson, the Secretary of State for External Affairs, made a speech on April 10, 1951 that caused some anger south of the border. He suggested that although United States-Canadian relations were close and growing closer, they would not always be smooth.

> There will be difficulties and frictions. These, however, will be easier to settle if the United States realizes that while we are most anxious to work with her and support her in the leadership she is giving to the free world, we are not willing to be merely an echo of somebody else's voice. It would be easier also if it were recognized by the United States at this time that we in Canada have had our own experience of tragedy and suffering and loss in war. In our turn, we should be careful not to transfer the suspicions and touchiness and hesitations of yesteryear from London to Washington.

. . . We must convince the United States by action rather than merely by word that we are, in fact, pulling our weight on this international team. But this does not mean that we should be told that until we do one twelfth or one sixteenth or some other fraction as much as they are doing in any particular enterprise, we are defaulting. It would also help if the United States took more notice of what we *do* do, and, indeed, occasionally of what we say. It is disconcerting, for example, that about the only time the American people seem to be aware of our existence, in contrast, say, to the existence of a Latin American republic, is when we do something they do not like, or do not do something which they would like.[12]

Even such mild reproofs were, however, seldom offered and Canada, led in later years by this same Lester Pearson, dutifully followed the American lead and integrated its defense policy with that of the United States in both the military and economic fields. It is difficult to say which better demonstrates the degree to which Canada, albeit with constant pressure from Washington, voluntarily tied itself to the United States in what has often been termed a "junior partnership in the Cold War." In 1951, the same year that the United States as a result of the Korean War was transforming its economy from a postwar to a Cold War economy, Canada also plunged into what might be termed a semi-war economy. That year Canada spent about $2 billion on defense. Although it did build some airplanes and produce some electronic equipment, Canada's role in the 1950s was to concentrate on the production of basic materials such as steel, nickel, and aluminum that a United States report had concluded were needed for the American defense effort. Thus, a major decision affecting Canada's economy was made in Washington, although executed with the concurrence of Ottawa.

Just as the Korean War brought a boom to the United States, so did it to Canada. The Minister of Defence, Brooke Claxton, declared that "Defence has become today the biggest single industry in Canada." During only nine months, the Canadian Commercial Corporation entered into eighty thousand defense contracts.[13] The boom, that stretched from 1950 to 1957, was the greatest in Canadian history.

> The stimulus for the boom of the 1950s came wholly from the United States, with the result that the east-west structure of the Canadian economy was fundamentally modified by an almost massive north-south integration. Toward the end of the period Canadian trade statistics revealed the emergence of almost entirely new exports to the U.S. of iron ore, uranium, oil, and nonferrous metals which rivaled and in some cases superseded in size the traditional staples which were sold in overseas markets.[14]

So too were Canada's military decisions dependent on those already made in Washington. United States military men saw a need for radar defenses against possible attacks from the Soviet Union across Canada and persuaded Canada to permit the construction of three radar networks between 1951 and 1957. A critic of Canadian defense policy has written: "Elaborate provisions regarding Canadian sovereignty were included . . ., but in effect Canada was reduced to providing the real estate while the United States provided the policy."[15]

An even more important decision was made in 1957. Washington convinced Ottawa that the Royal Canadian Air Force should be integrated into a North American Air Defense Comand (NORAD) with headquarters in Colorado Springs. Although Canada would be consulted, command would rest with American officers. This would almost inevitably mean that Canada would have little choice but to go along with an American decision to engage in hostilities, either defensively in response to a Soviet attack on the United States or even perhaps, in certain circumstances, offensively. This latter possibility arose during the Cuban missile crisis of 1962. NORAD ordered that all continental air forces, Canadian as well as American, be put on alert. John Diefenbaker, then the Canadian prime minister, refused for forty-eight hours to sanction the alert but Canadian forces went on the alert anyway. Five years later an American official recalled, "It wasn't as bad as it looked. This was because the Canadian forces went on full alert despite their government."[16] That is not to say that Canadian forces would necessarily have participated in an American attack on the Soviet missile sites in Cuba, being planned as a real possibility by the Kennedy administration.[17] But it did demonstrate the degree to which Ottawa's control of its own military forces had been weakened.

Controversy over Canada's defense policy was a substantial factor in the defeat of John Diefenbaker's government in 1963. Diefenbaker had come to power in 1957 when his Conservative party won a narrow victory. There were a number of factors contributing to the defeat of the Liberals but possibly the most important was that after twenty-two consecutive years in power "it was time for a change." Although the Conservatives won more seats than the Liberals, they could not form a majority government since nearly fifty seats had been won by two minor parties, the Cooperative Commonwealth Federation (a party with radical roots to the left of the Liberals) and the Social Credit party, to the right of the Conservatives. Finding it difficult to rule with a minority government, Diefenbaker called another election for 1958. The Liberals were disorganized, not yet solidly behind their new leader, Lester Pearson, and out of power in every provincial government except Newfoundland. Besides, the Canadians seemed to feel that the new government should be given sufficient support to be able to rule effectively. Diefenbaker had, by this time, turned into an effective politician. Canadians liked the old-fashioned eloquence with which he called for closer ties to Britain and the Commonwealth and less dependence on the United States. Too, he proclaimed a "vision" of the Canadian North bringing great prosperity to the nation. Whatever the reason, Diefenbaker received the greatest parliamentary majority in the history of Canada: 208 seats in a House of 265. The once-powerful Liberals won only 49 seats, the CCF only 8, and Social Credit not a one.

With such backing it would seem that Diefenbaker could achieve almost anything, but strangely things seemed to go wrong almost from the beginning. Perhaps Diefenbaker was a better politician than statesman; perhaps the Conservatives after so many years in the wilderness had forgotten how to govern; perhaps circumstances conspired against him. Certainly two aspects of Canadian-American relations did him serious political harm. One of the problems was financial. Although too complicated for anything but a brief summation, it can be said that the economic boom of the '50s petered out toward the end of the decade. With rising unemployment and economic stagnation, two factions of the ruling Conservative party argued about solutions in bitter, public disputes that came to be called "one of the most incredible public brawls in Canadian political history."[18] One of the questions involved in the dispute was the rising degree of American investment in Canadian industry. Even then some Canadians were beginning to argue that Canada was losing control of its economy to foreign investors, mainly American.

Diefenbaker also got involved in trade disputes with London and Washington. He was against Britain's joining the European Common Market but advanced no specific proposals for increasing Commonwealth trade. Nor did Diefenbaker respond favorably to President

Kennedy's suggestions for expanding world trade. Granted it was difficult for Canada to determine a trade policy for dealing with such giants as the Common Market and the United States, but Diefenbaker's government gave the impression of floundering. He angered the British government and Kennedy made little attempt to conceal his low esteem of Diefenbaker, even more for his military policy — or lack of one — than his trade policy.

It was probably the open dispute between Washington and Ottawa over defense matters that caused Diefenbaker the most political damage. Canada had decided in the early '50s to develop and manufacture its own supersonic jet fighter, the CF-105 (Arrow). By 1959, when Canada had spent several hundred millions on the project, it discovered that it had to drop it because the United States and NATO countries had decided not to buy any, claiming that they were not suitable. Canada itself would not require enough to justify continuing the program. So the highly skilled team of designers, engineers, and technicians was broken up, most of them going to California for jobs in the American aerospace program. This was a terrible blow to Canadian pride and the tendency was to blame the United States. Such blame was not entirely fair. Although, to be sure, the United States had led Canada into the Cold War military buildup, Canada had gone willingly.

The failure of the Arrow program did not cause the Canadian government to consider dropping out of the

Cold War competition. Rather it decided to purchase American jet fighters and the new Bomarc missile system. This latter decision was to have serious consequences for the Diefenbaker government. Although most Canadians had willingly supported American foreign policy at the time of the Korean War, as the decade wore on there was an increase in neutralist sentiment. Canada's attempt to find a defense role had been frustrating; it had increased interest in serving as a mediator in international disputes — a role difficult to justify as the intimate ally of one of two great Cold War powers — and many Canadians were beginning to question United States foreign policy. The U-2 spy planes' flights over the Soviet Union, the exile invasion of Cuba at the Bay of Pigs launched by the Kennedy administration, the feeling that the United States put too much stress on military considerations, all this encouraged neutralist sentiment in Canada. It was, no doubt, only a minority sentiment because most Canadians, like their government, saw no alternative to close association with the United States. But this sentiment existed in influential academic and intellectual circles.

Under these various circumstances Diefenbaker chose to face a national election in 1962. The voters were not quite disappointed enough to throw him out of office, but his party's astounding showing of four years before was cut almost in half, from 208 to 116. The Liberals doubled their total, from 49 to 100, and the minor parties revived. The New Democratic party (successor to the CCF) rose from 8 to 19, and Social Credit rebounded amazingly, soaring from no seats to 30. The Conservatives maintained power but once again were a minority government.

The election of a minority government — whose rule in a parliamentary system is almost always shaky — was the last straw for an economy already in trouble. The value of the Canadian dollar fell even further. Diefenbaker had to institute austerity measures and had to turn to the United States for large financial credits. ". . . above all, although the United States had been most generous and understanding at the height of the emergency, the terms of the settlement involved yet another servitude to the rich and powerful neighbor."[19]

From the economic crisis to a defense crisis. Bomarc missile sites had been constructed in Ontario and Quebec in 1961-62 but Diefenbaker had not yet decided whether or not to arm the missiles with nuclear warheads. He tried to temporize on the issue by saying that if a situation ever arose in which they were needed, they could quickly be obtained from the United States. This was not a very convincing response, for few believed that modern nuclear warfare, if ever it erupted, would permit sufficient time for the missiles to receive their nuclear warheads. The problem was that Diefenbaker did not know what to do. His Cabinet was divided. The Defence Minister argued that the Canadian forces should be fully equipped for any combat role that might be necessary in North America or Europe. The Secretary of State for External Affairs, Diefenbaker's closest associate, argued that Canada might be able to play an influential part in the important nuclear disarmament discussions under way if it did not undercut its political and moral position by becoming a member of the nuclear club. It must be remembered that this was at a time when there was widespread concern in the world about the effects of nuclear testing and warfare.

And there was more to it than that. Many authorities argued that the Bomarc missiles were obsolete or soon would be. Further, if Canada allowed nuclear missiles on Canadian soil, it would suffer the consequent criticism without having control over these weapons. American law mandated that such control remain in American hands and the talk of a "two-key" procedure was not very reassuring to some.

During 1962 Washington officially kept silent while behind the scenes it continued to pressure Diefenbaker into allowing nuclear warheads on the Bomarcs. Unofficially, however, Washington was not so silent and news stories surfaced every now and then betraying United States bafflement, even impatience. What was the point of having Bomarcs without nuclear warheads? The Cuban missile crisis increased the tension. Although President Kennedy had brought the world to the brink of nuclear warfare with his ultimatum to the Soviet Union to remove the missiles, he was seen in Canada, as in the United States, as a triumphant hero. And somehow Diefenbaker was seen by his own countrymen as one who had failed to give Kennedy the support he deserved. The reader should not be distressed by the inconsistency here. Canadians have often swung widely, and rapidly, from praise to condemnation of this or that American action. Then in January 1963 the retiring commander of NATO, American General Lauris Norstad, held a press conference in Ottawa in which he said it was his understanding that Canada had committed itself to acquiring nuclear warheads. A few days later, back in Washington, he said that NATO would suffer without a Canadian nuclear force. On January 12 the leader of the opposition, Liberal Lester Pearson, finally announced his views on the matter. He argued that Canada "should discharge its commitments . . . by accepting nuclear weapons for those defensive tactical weapons which cannot be effectively used without them."[20]

Diefenbaker, clearly on the defensive now, argued in Parliament that while Canada would cooperate with its allies, "she will not be a pawn nor be pushed around by other nations to do those things, which, in the opinion of the Canadian people, are not in keeping with her sovereignty." In any case, he said that negotiations had "been going on quite forcibly . . . for two or three months . . . so that . . . in case of need nuclear warheads will be made readily available."[21]

Washington's response was extraordinary, more like the response to the statement of a hostile government than that of a close ally. The State Department on January 30 made public a statement "which contained the bluntest rebuke to a Canadian prime minister ever made by the United States government."[22] The statement asserted that "the Canadian Government has not as yet proposed any arrangement sufficiently practical to contribute effectively to North American defense" and it went on to contradict directly several of Diefenbaker's statements.

The statement landed like a bombshell in Ottawa. All the political parties joined in protesting what Diefenbaker called "an unwarranted intrusion" in Canadian affairs.[23] This normally would have been a most effective response except that Kennedy was estraordinarily popular in Canada and Diefenbaker was already in political trouble, not only for his indecisiveness on the Bomarcs but because of economic and other problems. Several of his Cabinet ministers tried to get him to resign. When that failed, the Defence Minister resigned. The Liberals saw their opportunity and called for a vote of "no confidence" in the Parliament. The Liberals were joined by the members of the minor parties and for the second time since Confederation in 1867 a government fell on a no-confidence vote.

Some leading Conservatives tried to purge Diefenbaker, but he fought back tenaciously and routed his intra-party foes. Yet the political toll was great. Some of his ministers resigned and some refused to run for reelection. When the campaign began, Conservative newspapers and businessmen deserted. In his campaign speeches Diefenbaker said that everyone was against him but the people and he accused the Liberals of taking their orders from south of the border. This latter tactic was not very productive in view of Kennedy's enormous popularity. On the other hand, Diefenbaker was not as badly hurt by the missile controversy as might have been expected, for there were many Canadians who were not eager to possess nuclear weapons. This was particularly true in Quebec where the French-Canadians were still distrustful of committing Canada to the defense of other countries. And Quebec, as we have often seen, was the very heart of liberal country where Pearson's party needed to score heavily.

Despite the terrible disarray of the Conservatives, the Liberals were able to win only a minority victory, capturing 129 House seats, four short of a majority. The minor parties and the Conservatives had no taste for another election, however, so the Pearson government retained a precarious but somehow durable grip. Washington welcomed Lester Pearson's victory. He had long been popular in the United States. He was pro-American, seemed in many ways like an American, was a passionate follower of American baseball and was skillful in cultivating the American press. Because of his work at the UN, he was a frequent visitor to New York and Washington and he had enormous prestige because of the Nobel Peace Prize he had won in 1957 for his work in establishing the UN Emergency Force that patrolled the Egyptian-Israeli border to prevent another outbreak of fighting after the Suez War of 1956. Familiar with many members of the Kennedy administration, he soon developed a close relationship with the President and, for a while, with President Johnson. Pearson, despite the growing criticism in Canada, supported American foreign policy, including even the invasion of the Dominican Republic to put down a popular revolution aimed to restore to power the democratically elected president, Juan Bosch. And in 1967, with opposition to the Vietnam War growing in Canada as it was in the United States, Pearson refused to ban the sale of arms for use in Vietnam. Asked to do so by a group of professors at the University of Toronto, he said:

> It is clear that the imposition of an embargo on the export of military equipment to the United States, and concomitant termination of the Production Sharing Agreements, would have far-reaching consequences which no Canadian Government would contemplate with equanimity. It would be interpreted as a notice of withdrawal on our part from continental defense and even the collective defense arrangements of the Atlantic Alliance.[24]

This demonstrates the degree of closeness, amounting even to dependence, critics have argued, between the policies of Canada and the United States. Yet, as we shall see, time would create a divergence of Canadian foreign policy, based largely on the developing opposition, wider and deeper, to the Vietnam War.

10

Two Canadas — or One?

UP TO THIS POINT, the writer has taken a fairly strict chronological course, but now it is necessary to change, for we have reached contemporary Canada, and its problems are so complex that, even though they are interwoven, we must try to consider them separately if we are to make some sense of them. French-Canadian *separatisme* is related to the concern over American investments in Canada which is in turn related to the growing Canadian nationalism, and the problem of federal-provincial relations is involved with all three.

Looking at Canada through these problems is only one way of viewing that enormous nation to the north. There is another way, to use the words of George Woodcock in his splendid book, *Canada and the Canadians*. He sees it this way:

> Canada today is a rich country scarred by poverty, a democracy governed and controlled by élites restricted by class, race and creed. It is a land where legal discrimination does not exist, but where the fact of being a Catholic or an Indian or the child of a poor family may have a considerable and detrimental effect on one's future. It is a land of disparities, regional and human.[1]

Such words come close to describing the United States. Canada, too, is a rich country, vying with Sweden for the honor of having the highest standard of living in the world after the United States. But standard of living is more a statistical than a real concept. These statistics can obscure the fact that in both Canada and the United States, despite the tables and graphs and charts showing how well that *per capita* person lives, there are unconscionable numbers of human beings living in or near dire poverty. There are great numbers in both nations discriminated against because of the accident of birth; there are great numbers who do not have the equal opportunity that is supposed to be their birthright. Yet in neither country are these humane obligations met as resolutely as they should be, for it is the nature of societies to be diverted from primary tasks. In the United States the diversions in recent years have been the war in Vietnam and, more recently, the state of the economy. Perhaps when those things have been set right the nation, unless it finds other diversions, will turn to those for whom help is not only necessary but obligatory. So, too, with Canada. It has urgent tasks but it seems unable to give them the necessary attention until it has settled, permanently or temporarily, the problems of ethnic division and of getting along with its overpowering southern neighbor.

A pessimistic Canadian might be hard pressed to say which he thinks more dangerous: the possibility of an internal collapse caused by the secession of the aggrieved French-Canadians of Quebec Province; or the possibility of the economic, or even political, absorption of Canada by the United States. There is good reason to believe that neither will happen but there are many serious, well-informed, calm Canadians who think either or both a genuine possibility. And even if the extreme does not happen, both can continue to cause grievous difficulty for Canada.

The older problem, and the more dramatic since the kidnapping of a British diplomat and the kidnap-murder of a provincial official in October 1970, is the relations between the French- and English-Canadians. The problem goes all the way back to the English conquest of Quebec in 1759 which established British rule over a French community already more than a century old. Since that time the English- and the French-Canadians have lived side by side for more than two centuries and yet neither community has made much effort to know and understand the other. The English—or so it seems to an outsider—have made even less effort to understand than the French. Perhaps, quite humanly, they felt they didn't have to. After all, they had won the battle for Canada and, later, they were the majority in a democracy. Also, they genuinely regarded themselves as the progressive force in Canada, while the conservative French-Canadians with their devotion to the Church and the land moved slowly and reluctantly into modern times. Furthermore, the English-Canadians, as we saw, genuinely believed that the French-Canadians did not pull their weight in the two world wars—weren't patriotic enough.

The French-Canadians, however, saw it entirely differently. They were the real Canadian patriots. Their ties to France had been cut a century before Confederation in 1867. Their only loyalty was to Canada; they weren't like the English-Canadians with their divided loyalty to Canada and Britain. They remembered that Canada was first a French country, that the glories of Canadian history were French, that their people, unlike so many other Canadians, were not newcomers. They had been there for centuries. They also knew that many English looked down on them as backward and inferior and scorned the church to which they were devoted. They knew that their language, the first language of

Canada, was a foreign language in most of the country, that all opportunities were open to the English speaker and only a few to the French, that many English speakers lived their entire lives in French-speaking communities and never bothered to learn the language, expecting the French-Canadians to deal with them in English. They knew that the economic life of Canada, even French Canada, was dominated by the English. Most of all the French wanted to be treated as equals. They fully recognized that they were not numerically equal but they believed to the depth of their beings that it was not merely a matter of numbers, even in a democracy, that the French as a nation were equal to the English as a nation and should be respected and treated as such. But for some reason most English-Canadians could not understand this unshakable conviction of their French countrymen.

Although, as we have seen, French Canada would occasionally burst into political activity when it feared *la survivance* was threatened, the French-Canadians were not nearly so political a people as the English. Their life was carried out through church, school, and a multiplicity of social, civil, and fraternal organizations. Politics were pretty much left to the politicians — and the priests. In Quebec, the only province with a French majority, government was more concerned with preserving and strengthening the French tradition. Although there were occasionally French-Canadian political fig-

ures who were important on the national stage (Laurier
and St. Laurent were, of course, prime ministers), very
few top cabinet posts were held by French-Canadians.
Usually the members of Parliament were most concerned with representing the province's views at Ottawa
and trying to rally support in Quebec for their party. In
provincial politics, Quebec's leaders were most concerned, after insuring *la survivance*, with the distribution
of patronage and getting along with the English-speaking leaders of the financial community in Montreal.
Maurice Duplessis, long the boss of Quebec Province,
was generally recognized as corrupt and was not reluctant to use the police to end strikes by French-Canadians
against English businessmen.

During the 1950s in Quebec, as all over the world,
people who felt themselves mistreated began to feel also
that they should do something about it. These people,
mainly younger members of the middle class, often in-
tellectuals and academics, shared the conviction of their
elders that French-Canadians had to protect their identity. But they also came to feel that the traditional French-
Canadian way of life had handicapped the people. The
conservative schools, they were convinced, had not prepared French-Canadians to take their place in modern
society. The French could hardly hope to compete with
the English if their schools concentrated solely on pro-
ducing priests and lawyers. They must produce men and
women who could work on the newspapers, in broad-

casting stations, banks, business, industry — the whole
range of skills essential to present-day society. But such
change would be possible only if the old politicians and
the old priests (some younger priests, as in other parts of
the world, were among the most effective seekers of
change) could be forced to relinquish their power. On
the other hand, these traditional leaders were skilled and
convinced that the old ways were the best. It would not
be easy to displace them. The defeat of the old guard
was perhaps inevitable but would not necessarily happen
quickly. Fate intervened. Duplessis died in 1959. But
even this did not mean that his party, *Union Nationale*,
was finished. Unaccountably Duplessis's successor, Paul
Sauvé, began a vigorous program of reform. But then
he, too, died. Even that did not mean the collapse of the
Union Nationale. Such were the loyalties of Quebec's
conservative elements — the farmers, the small-town
businessmen, the old-fashioned parish priests, some
blue-collar workers, big business — that it remained a
potent political force. The provincial Liberal party, even
though reinvigorated under Jean Lesage, won a narrow
victory of merely five hundred votes spread over five
constituencies.

Once change came, however, it came rapidly. The
educational system was drastically reorganized with
power being removed from the hands of the Church.
These new provincial Liberals were also reformist in
almost every field, providing a time of ferment. The

ideas of radical and socialist thinkers were welcomed, and sometimes adopted. Among the most influential of these young thinkers was a lawyer-teacher, Pierre Elliott Trudeau, co-editor of the radical *Cité Libre*, whose influence was much greater than its tiny circulation.

Most English-Canadians welcomed the end of Quebec's rule by the conservative *Union Nationale*. They assumed that more modern French-Canadians would be more like them, more sympathetic to the views of English Canada. They were wrong. These new French-Canadians were modern, to be sure, but they were just as French as their elders. Indeed, many of them were not content to be merely on the defensive. Ideas abounded that still continue to be discussed. All of them were based on the general conviction that change in the status of French Canada was necessary. Some of them were mutually exclusive and many others overlapped. The most modest required that Quebec's powers be increased and that the rights of French-Canadians in the rest of Canada be strengthened. Some advocated giving Quebec a status different from that of the other provinces. This view had gradations ranging from modest changes to almost separate nationhood. Others said that Quebec should be a separate or semi-separate state associated with Canada in a loose federation or through an economic union. And still others argued that Quebec should be a separate nation in every sense. But while separatists are numerous in Quebec (René Levesque's

Parti Québeçois received twenty-three percent of the vote in the spring of 1970 on a platform of political independence with close economic ties to English Canada), they are not nearly so numerous outside the province. French-Canadians, who make up significant minorities in Ontario, New Brunswick and, to a lesser degree, Nova Scotia, fear that they would be almost powerless in a Canada without Quebec. They would lose powerful political allies and English-Canadians would have less reason to accommodate a people who would suddenly have become almost aliens. These French-Canadians, and many in Quebec, believed that the Canadian Constitution should be amended to provide not only individual rights but collective rights (*droits collectifs*) as well. They point to the fact that the English in Quebec have guaranteed rights (in a workable system) while the French in English provinces do not.

When Lester Pearson and the federal Liberals came into power in 1963, Pearson demonstrated great concern over the discontent in Quebec. He immediately tried to be responsive to the feelings of the province. Quebec was, of course, essential to the Liberal party; besides, Pearson feared that an unresponsive federal government would cause more extremist views to gain increased support. He immediately instituted measures to get more French-Canadians in the federal civil service and to encourage the learning and use of French within the federal government. A new flag (the maple leaf) was adopted in place of the old one that prominently displayed the British Union Jack. Most important, Pearson established a Royal Commission on Bilingualism and Biculturalism. It had a distinguished membership of four English and four French representatives plus two Canadians of other ethnic backgrounds. In 1965 the Commission issued a preliminary report in which the members declared:

> We believe that there is a crisis, in the sense that Canada has come to a time when decisions must be taken and developments must occur leading either to its break-up, or to a new set of conditions for its future existence. We do not know whether the crisis will be short or long. We are convinced that it is here. The signs of danger are many and serious.[2]

And they warned:

> There are those who feel that the problems will lessen and go away with time. This is possible, but in our view, it is more probable that unless there are major changes the situation will worsen with time, and that it could worsen much more quickly than many think.[3]

The Commission had discovered that *not a single French-Canadian* they had talked to was content with his particular situation or with the status of the French people in Canada.

While it might seem at first that some English-Canadians might say "good riddance" to Quebec, its independence would be a severe blow to Canada. Quebec is rich in human and material resources; furthermore, it is a physical link between the Maritime Provinces and cen-

tral and western Canada. And the St. Lawrence Sea-
way — a joint United States-Canadian project opened in
1959 — runs mainly through Quebec. Perhaps even more
important is another possible consequence of Quebec's
secession: "But the dissension between French and English Canada was only one among many divisions . . .
and even the most conservative of politicians and political observers began to consider seriously the consequences of fragmentation of the country that might not
end with the secession of Quebec."[4]

While some of English Canada thought Pearson was
making too many concessions to Quebec, some Quebeckers thought these concessions were mere "token-
ism," to use the language of black militants in the United States. Such an identification is not gratuitous, for the
more militant separatists have argued that the French-
Canadians are the "white niggers of America," the name
given to a powerful and disturbing book written by
Pierre Vallières, one of the most prominent members of
the *Front de Libération du Québec* (FLQ).

The vigorous development in Quebec in the 1960s
has been termed *la révolution tranquille* but the times
were not always quiet. Early in the decade a genuine
revolutionary movement began to develop in Quebec.
Its origins are not quite clear. Some credit, or blame, has
been given to Algeria and Cuba but the degree of responsibility of those revolutionary governments is far
from clear. In any case, a number of Quebeckers, aug-

mented perhaps by a few foreigners, were determined to establish a true revolutionary movement, with resort to violence if necessary. They were impatient with the revolutionary efforts of the French-Canadian reformers, socialists, and radicals who pursued non-violent means. One can understand their impatience, for a severe economic downturn was added to all the other grievances. Quebec, like the rest of Canada, suffered from inflation but even worse was its rate of unemployment, the highest in Canada, a condition that still exists and has, indeed, worsened at the time this is written. Nevertheless, while such impatience can be understood, it is harder to understand why the FLQ resorted to violence while both the federal and provincial governments were making genuine efforts to find a satisfactory solution to the legitimate grievances of French Canada. At first the violence was minor—a series of mailbox bombings in the prosperous English surburb of Westmount at the edge of Montreal. But they soon grew more serious, as an army explosives expert was maimed for life and, a short time later, an old watchman was killed in a dynamite explosion at a downtown Montreal armory. Some of these terrorists were captured and sent to prison in disgrace, for their melodramatics had not resulted in any great increase in support.

By the end of 1963 Quebec, and Canada, thought the terrorism was over. After all, it was hardly characteristic of the placid Canadian society. But on August 29, 1964 five members of the FLQ attempted to hold up Montreal's largest weapons store. The manager was killed by a panicky robber and an employee was mistakenly killed by police. On May 5, 1966 a bomb was placed in a Montreal shoe factory which had been involved in a long and bitter labor dispute. A woman clerk was killed and eight others wounded. Two months later a terrorist was killed by a bomb that exploded before it was placed at a textile plant. There was then a long pause in major incidents until December 1968, when the homes of two Montreal businessmen were bombed. In February 1969 a bomb exploded in the visitors' gallery of the new Montreal Stock Exchange, injuring twenty-seven persons. A few months later a bomb exploded in the home of Montreal's mayor, Jean Drapeau, and terrorists exploded twelve sticks of dynamite in Ottawa at the National Defence Communications Centre, killing a fifty-year-old woman employee.

Although all of these inexcusable incidents were attributed to, or claimed by, the FLQ, it is impossible to know whether they were the result of a planned, coordinated campaign or sporadic acts of violence by individuals or small groups acting more or less independently. While it seems certain that a fairly substantial number of Quebeckers had a certain sympathy for the FLQ, it also seems certain that it has never had more than a small active membership, perhaps as many as two thousand (the highest estimate) but quite possibly only a fraction of that.[5] In any case, the number prepared to carry out armed attacks must have been much smaller still—130, according to one source.[6] This out of a population of some six million in Quebec. Obviously, the FLQ had not achieved the very basic requisite for a revolutionary movement, the support of the people.

Before turning to the terrible events of October 1970 that shocked the Canadian people and captured the world's attention, it is necessary to look briefly at developments that form a vital context. The French-Canadian question continued to dominate the considerations of Lester Pearson's ruling Liberal party but for a while in 1967 the issue quieted down. All Canada was engaged in the celebration of the nation's centennial, marked by the superb Expo 67 constructed on two islands in the St. Lawrence. The selection of the great city of French Canada, Montreal, as its site and the national cooperation that marked its planning, construction, and operation seemed to demonstrate that Canada was indeed one nation, for both French- and English-Canadians took enormous, and justified, pride in Expo 67. But then in July of that year, as part of the centennial celebration, President Charles de Gaulle of France came to Quebec Province. He did not confine himself to the ritualistic pleasantries customary to such occasions; instead, he emphasized the ties between France and Quebec and even, to the horror of most English-Canadians and to the joy of most French-Canadians, uttered these special words, *"Vive le Québec libre,"* the slogan of the French separatists. Lester Pearson declared that such intervention in a domestic matter was "inadmissible," so the haughty Frenchman returned to Paris without visiting the capital of the nation whose centennial he had come to help celebrate. Almost all historians and commentators agree that De Gaulle's visit had great impact. Ramsay Cook, a young Canadian historian, put it this way:

> When, in a few decades, historians turn to analysing the long, controversial career of the General, the place allotted to Canada and Quebec will almost certainly be small. But when, twenty years hence, historians turn to writing about Canada and Quebec in 1967, the visit of the French President will almost certainly be judged an event of substantial significance. Whatever General De Gaulle's ambiguous motives may have been, and whatever definitive interpretation is placed upon his now famous "Vive le Québec libre," there can be no doubt that his adventures in "la nouvelle France" finally brought into focus the fundamental nature of the current Canadian crisis. The General, of course, did not create that crisis. Nor, in the long run, can he even be said to have exacerbated it. What he did, in his characteristically histrionic fashion, was to simplify and dramatize the fact that this country has arrived at the point where the crisis of survival is so serious that sides much be chosen, serious and official discussions set afoot, and a new accommodation reached.[7]

At the end of 1967 Lester Pearson, seeing signs that his Liberal party was losing ground to the reviving Conservatives, made a shrewd move. He resigned in December and his place was taken, not by a familiar Liberal face, but by a French-Canadian almost unknown outside his province. He was Pierre Elliot Trudeau, dark, attractive, a bachelor who admired good-looking women and fast cars. In short, he brought glamour to the drab Canadian politics. But he was not chosen merely because he gave promise of being a good television campaigner. He was a trained economist and a lawyer. He had been a university teacher and he had demonstrated his concern for and knowledge of social and political matters by his editorship of the influential magazine, *Cité Libre*. He had been a socialist, even a radical, but in recent years he had drifted away from the leftist New Democratic party to the Liberals. His admirers have said he made the change in the conviction that reform was more possible in the Liberal party than with the New Democrats. His detractors have said the move was prompted by political ambition.

Trudeau joined the Liberals in 1965. The next year he, along with two colleagues, Jean Marchand and Gérard Pelletier, was elected to Parliament, meaning that "for the first time for a decade, the federal government included a group of French-Canadians who were men of brilliant intelligence, strong convictions and forceful personalities, and who were in no way compromised by the errors of the past."[8] Pearson was grateful, for their presence did much to lessen the suspicions of French Canada. The three were promoted quickly, Trudeau becoming Minister of Justice in 1967. He immediately drew up bills amending the Criminal Code in a number of ways, including more liberal provisions relating to sexual behavior. Explaining his reforms to the press, he declared, "There's no place for the state in the bedrooms of the nation," a statement that was repeated the nation over.

The Liberals met in April 1968 and chose Trudeau as their leader, meaning he replaced the retiring Pearson as prime minister. He quickly called an election for June and the Liberals won easily, gaining 155 seats to 72 for the Conservatives, 22 for the NDP, with 14 *Créditistes* and 1 independent. Canada was eager for a fresh, young face after the interminable political wrangles of the old politicians. They wanted someone who might offer some new solutions to old problems and a French-Canadian particularly seemed to be the right man to deal with the ancient, intractable problem of his people's role in Canadian life. His own people clearly had faith in him. Although the separatists had called for massive abstentions, the Liberals won 55 out of Quebec's 74 seats.

Trudeau is clearly not a separatist. Although very much a French-Canadian, he believes that Quebec's place is within the Canadian federation and without any great constitutional changes. He has attempted to educate English Canada to understand the French grievances and he has intensified Pearson's program of bilingualism. Within the last couple of years the provincial legislatures of Ontario, New Brunswick, and Manitoba (home of three-quarters of the non-Quebec French-Canadians) have provided for public schools in which French is the language of instruction, sometimes over the bitter protests of English speakers who are somehow angered by the fact that most French-Canadians want to retain their French culture.

Even the fact of a French-Canadian prime minister has not been able to deflate the separatist movement in Quebec. It is certainly a minority (only about a quarter of the voters supported it in 1970), but most of the rest of the people of Quebec share the conviction that something should be done, preferably inside the Canadian federation, to improve the place of the French-Canadian. Severe economic difficulties in the province have emphasized this feeling. But no one expected the shocking events of October 1970.

Just before 8:30 on the morning of October 5 two armed men, announcing themselves as members of the FLQ, burst past a maid and kidnapped James Cross, the 49-year-old British Trade Commissioner in Montreal. They hurried him past a third armed man outside the door and into a cab driven by a fourth. It would be sixty days before he was found — safe.

The kidnappers soon got a message to Montreal police. In return for the release of Cross they wanted: the release of twenty-three "political prisoners" (men who had been jailed for bombings or terrorist incidents); a chartered plane to take them to Algeria or Cuba; a press escort to ensure their safety; a $500,000 "voluntary tax" in gold bullion; and publication of the name and photograph of a man who was supposed to have informed, thus breaking up a cell that planned the kidnapping of the U.S. consul-general. They also demanded publication in all Quebec newspapers of a manifesto setting forth the FLQ program; the reinstatement of several hundred truck drivers who had been laid off by the government; and the total end of police attempts to locate the kidnappers.

These demands presented the provincial and federal government with a terrible dilemma. In a kidnapping for ransom, the money can be paid and the person returned. That's the end of it. But one successful political kidnapping often begets another, as demonstrated in recent years in Latin America. On the other hand, there was a human life involved, the representative of Canada's mother country. The kidnappers said there would be only forty-eight hours to decide. Since the hostage was a guest of the federal government, Quebec waived its jealously guarded prerogatives and appealed to Ottawa for direction. Trudeau called his cabinet into session. He made the decisions but he designated Mitchell Sharp, the Minister of External Affairs, to be the government's spokesman. Sharp termed the demands "unreasonable," adding, "I need hardly say that this set of demands will not be met." This perhaps implied a willingness to negotiate on other demands.

The government's tough reply set off a series of postponed execution dates and reduced demands delivered to

French-language radio stations. An anonymous phone caller would tell the station where the latest note was hidden: in a phone booth or in a pile of rubbish or under a doormat somewhere. A reporter would rush out for the note, rush back to his studio and read it on the air, informing the public before the humiliated police and government. By Thursday, October 8, it was clear there would be no quick police solution to the kidnapping. (Indeed, the police manhunt has been termed inept and blundering by many commentators.) That night the FLQ scored its first victory. Its manifesto was broadcast. It was an extraordinary document, calling not only for some changes but for an entire transformation of the society along anarcho-socialist lines. The manifesto also named as those most to blame for Quebec's problems a number of politicians and business leaders, many of whom quickly fled town.

As a reward for reading the manifesto, the kidnappers removed any specific deadline for Cross's death and dropped most of their earlier demands. All they still demanded was the transportation of the twenty-three political prisoners to Algeria or Cuba and an end to the police investigation. By this time the federal government had turned the matter back to the provincial authorities. The man in charge was Quebec's Minister of Justice, Jerome Choquette. His moment of relaxation did not last long for the FLQ then sent another message, saying that Cross would be executed if the prisoners were not released by Saturday at 6 P.M. Shortly before the deadline Choquette went on the air and, speaking in both French and English, said no deal would be made. "No society can expect that the decisions of its governments or of its courts of law can be questioned or can be erased by the use of blackmail exercised by a group, because this signifies the end of all social order. It is the negation of the freedom of individuals and groups."[9]

The only concessions the Quebec government would make were these: consideration of the kidnappers' claims of injustices within the society; "objective consideration" of parole for the twenty-three prisoners; and safe conduct out of the country for the kidnappers if they returned Cross unharmed. "If, on the other hand, you choose to refuse such safe conduct, I can assure you that you will benefit before our courts of all possible clemency in view of any humanitarian gesture you make to spare the life of Mr. Cross. This I can assure you."

The weary justice minister left the studios at 6:15. A few minutes later an already anxious Canada heard that the deputy premier of Quebec, Pierre Laporte, had also been kidnapped. He had been playing football in a suburban street with a nephew. A car pulled up. Two men got out, one carrying an automatic rifle. In front of his horrified nephew, he was forced into the car beside another two or three men. No word came until the next morning, Sunday, at 9 A.M. Laporte would be killed at 10 P.M. that night unless the original demands made after the kidnapping of Cross were met. It seemed obvious that a different group, more militant than the first, had grabbed Laporte.

The tension throughout Canada, especially in Quebec, was terrible. The country, and even more the province, were in a state of shock. This sort of thing just didn't happen in Canada. But it had happened and the lives of two men were at stake. The young premier of Quebec, Robert Bourassa, faced an awful dilemma. If he did not make substantial concessions to the kidnappers, both men might die. If he did, there might be an epidemic of political kidnappings. His Cabinet was divided. Some members were willing to make concessions; others threatened to quit if substantial concessions were made.

A second ultimatum came and then, surprisingly, a third. This last one contained a handwritten note from Laporte. He was known to be a brave man and reportedly had advocated a hard line after the Cross kidnapping, but in his note he pleaded for his life. The restraint of his language made the appeal all the more moving.

My dear Robert,

1. I am convinced that I am writing the most important letter of my whole life;

2. For the moment I am in perfect health. I am well treated; even with courtesy;

3. I insist that the police cease all searches to find me. If they found me, this would culminate in a murderous gun battle from which I certainly would not emerge alive. This is absolutely crucial;

4. You have the power in effect to decide as to my life. If it was only a matter of that and if this sacrifice could have good results, one might consider it. But we are faced with a well-organized escalation which will not end until the liberation of the "political prisoners." After me it will be a third then a fourth then a fifth person. If all politicians are protected, they will strike at other classes of society. Therefore act immediately and avoid a quite useless bloodbath and panic;

5. You know my personal case, which is worthy of attention. I had two brothers; they are both dead. I remain alone as the head of a large family which consists of my mother, my sisters, my own wife and my children, as well as the children of Roland [his brother] of whom I am the tutor. My departure would mean irreparable grief, for you know the closeness which unites the members of my family. It is not only I who am implicated, but a dozen persons, all of them women and young children. I believe you understand!

6. If the departure of the "political prisoners" is organized and brought to a satisfactory conclusion, I am certain my personal safety will be absolute — mine, and that of the others who might follow me.

7. This could be done rapidly, for I don't see why, by taking more time about it, you would continue to make me die little by little in the place where I am held.

Decide — my life or my death. I am counting on you and thank you for it.

Regards,
Pierre Laporte

P.S. I repeat, have the searches ended. And don't let the police decide to continue without your knowledge. The success of this search would be a death warrant for me.[10]

This moving letter increased the pressure on Bourassa, not only for itself but for the impact it would have when made public. Bourassa did not want to give in, nor did he want the two hostages to die. Just before the ten o'clock deadline, he went on the radio and made a cleverly worded stalling speech: ". . . Before discussing the application of these demands, we want to establish mechanisms which would guarantee—to use Mr. Laporte's example—that the liberation of the prisoners would have as a definite result the safety of both hostages."[11] Without promising anything, Bourassa was asking for more time in a way the kidnappers would find difficult to resist.

The Liberation cell, which had Cross, decided first that the government was beginning to yield and gave their word they would release Cross unharmed, but said that they could not go into the details of release without compromising their own security. Their reply was accompanied by a note from Cross saying that he trusted the kidnappers. When the Liberation reply was broadcast, the Chenier cell, which had Laporte, decided to go along, but they held out for all the original concessions. Both named Robert Lemieux, a lawyer often identified with the FLQ, as their spokesman and negotiator. Bourassa, in turn, named a 33-year-old corporation lawyer, Robert Demers, as the government negotiator. He wanted time, hoping the police could find the two hostages before a final decision had to be made.

Although Bourassa was in day-to-day charge of the situation, the federal prime minister was obviously equally concerned. Trudeau was outraged but there was little he could do for the moment. However, he and his

Cabinet decided to call up the army in Ottawa. Battle-ready soldiers with fixed bayonets took up positions outside Parliament, the prime minister's residence, and that of the governor-general. This alarmed the nation even more. The situation was that bad, this action seemed to say. Some people objected to calling up the army, among them a TV reporter who stopped Trudeau outside his office. An extraordinary interview resulted.

TV MAN: "My choice is to live in a society that is free and democratic which means that you don't have people with guns running around in it. And one of the things that I have to give up for that choice is the fact that people like you may be kidnapped."

THE PRIME MINISTER: "Well, there's a lot of bleeding hearts around that just don't like to see people with helmets and guns. All I can say is 'Go on and bleed.' But it's more important to keep law and order in society than to be worried about weak-kneed people who don't like the looks of any army."

TV MAN: "At any cost? How far would you go with that, how far would you extend that?"

PM: "Just watch me."

TV MAN: "At reducing civil liberties? To that extent?"

PM: "To what extent?"

TV MAN: "Well, if you extend this, and you say you're going to do anything to protect them, this could include wiretapping, reducing other liberties in some way."

PM: "Yes, I think that society must take every means

at its disposal to defend itself against the emergence of a parallel power which defies the elected power in this country, and I think that goes to any distance. So long as there is power here which is challenging the elected representatives of the people, then I think that power must be stopped and I think it's only, I repeat, weak-kneed bleeding hearts who are afraid to take those measures."[12]

Such a response from a man known for his dedication to civil liberties was a measure of the tension under which Prime Minister Trudeau was working. That this was not idle talk became clear within a couple of days.

It was Tuesday now and Lemieux and Demers got down to negotiations, but there was little they could negotiate. Lemieux said he could discuss only the implementation of the demands, not the demands themselves. Demers also said he could not discuss the demands, only the method that would ensure the safe return of the hostages if a later decision were made to meet some or all of the demands. Obviously, the two lawyers got nowhere. Nor did they do any better that night. Nevertheless, the feeling spread through Montreal that some sort of accommodation was in the making. Certainly a great many people in Quebec Province, although not condoning kidnapping, expressed sympathy with the goals of the FLQ.

By Thursday, October 15, the mood shifted again. Bourassa, addressing the provincial parliament in Quebec City, announced that he had asked the federal government to send troops to Montreal. Quickly a 200-

truck convoy left Ottawa for Montreal, and military transport planes carried men and supplies. By evening more than a thousand troops were in Montreal. And Quebec invoked the Police Act, an emergency law putting all police and army personnel in the province under the command of the director of the Quebec Provincial Police for thirty days. Thus, twelve thousand police and a thousand soldiers were at his disposal to maintain security and seek the kidnappers.

Montreal was quiet but tense. Time was obviously running out. At 9 o'clock that night, Thursday the 15th, Bourassa made an offer: there could be no question of freeing the twenty-three "political prisoners" or meeting any of the other demands. But the federal government was prepared to parole five of the prisoners and give the kidnappers safe conduct to a country of their choice. This was not much of an offer, for safe conduct had been offered at the beginning. Lemieux turned it down flat and went to a rally in the French-Canadian east end of Montreal where some 1,500 students were proclaiming their solidarity with the FLQ.

Within a few hours Pierre Elliott Trudeau took the action over which there is controversy to this day. At exactly 4 A.M., Friday, October 16, the Prime Minister invoked, for the first time in Canada's peacetime history, the Emergency War Measures Act (WMA). In Parliament only Thomas Douglas, the leader of the New Democratic party, objected, saying, "The government, I submit, is using a sledgehammer to crack a peanut."

The War Measures Act permitted any police officer, federal, provincial or local, to search and arrest without warrant, to detain incommunicado arrested suspects for up to ninety days without bail and without charges being made for up to three weeks. And there is a wide range of prohibited action. Although most Canadians supported the invocation of the WMA, many because they believed an insurrection was possible, some harsh critics have argued that such extreme measures were unnecessary, that the threat to public safety was not of sufficient magnitude to justify such sweeping measures. However, in a speech broadcast that night, Prime Minister Trudeau said:

> I can assure you that the government is most reluctant to seek such powers and did so only when it became crystal clear that the situation could not be controlled unless some extraordinary assistance was made available on an urgent basis.
> The authority contained in the act will permit governments to deal effectively with the nebulous yet dangerous challenge to society represented by the terrorist organizations. The criminal law as it stands is simply not adequate to deal with systematic terrorism.[13]

By 11 o'clock on Friday morning, the police had arrested about 150 suspects: labor organizers, teachers, students, radical politicians, writers. Lemieux, the FLQ's negotiator, was among the first to be picked up. Eventually more than 400 persons were arrested, but the emergency powers were not restricted to Quebec Province. In Vancouver the mayor announced he might use the powers against radical groups, drug pushers, and Americans fleeing the draft. A student newspaper in Alberta, planning to print the manifesto of the FLQ merely as information so people could learn what the extremists wanted, had its plates seized. Newspapers all over the country imposed self-censorship. The people as a whole approved Trudeau's action and there were calls for national ID cards with photos and fingerprints, censorship of publications and broadcasts, a housecleaning of university faculties, and restraints on university students.

The next night radio station CKAC received a phone call which told of a communiqué and where it could be found. The worst had happened:

> Faced with the arrogance of the federal government and of its servant Bourassa, faced with their obvious bad faith, the FLQ has decided to start acting.
>
> Pierre Laporte, minister of unemployment and of assimilation, was executed at 6:18 tonight by the Dieppe Cell (Royal 22nd).
>
> You will find the body in the trunk of the green Chevrolet (9J2420) at the St. Hubert Base.
>
> We shall conquer.
>
> FLQ
>
> P.S. The exploiters of the Quebec people had better act properly.[14]

The body was found stuffed in the trunk of the car. As word of the cold-blooded murder was spread, the province and the nation were horrified. Peaceful, placid Canada had come to bloody violence. And even as the shock and grief and anger spread, there was the inevitable question: Was Cross still alive? He was, and on Sunday afternoon the FLQ released a letter from him saying he was still well. For the moment then the federal and provincial governments could concentrate on Laporte's funeral. His widow bitterly rejected the idea of a lavish state funeral. Perhaps she felt that the state could have done more to save his life. But the government insisted that the funeral be a big occasion, not only as a tribute to Laporte but as a gesture of defiance to the terrorists. The funeral on Tuesday, October 20, was unlike any other in Canadian history. There was a vast outpouring of political leaders from the prime minister down and a vast outpouring of private mourners — under a security umbrella unlike any even imagined in Canada until that day. Barricades, machine guns, fixed bayonets, sharpshooters on the roofs of tall buildings, even police dogs sniffing for dynamite in the magnificent Notre Dame Church — one of the most beautiful in the world.

Finally, on December 2, police tracked down the captors of James Cross. After some negotiating, they were allowed the next day to fly to asylum in Cuba. No one can know why they allowed Cross to live all that time. Maybe they had never intended to kill him, intending to use him solely for bargaining purposes. Maybe the murder of Laporte had sobered them. Whatever the reason, Cross was free, and a few weeks later the suspects in the murder of Laporte were captured at a farm about thirty miles outside Montreal.

It is difficult to reach firm conclusions about those terrible days of October. Some critics of the course taken by Trudeau and Bourassa have argued that the invocation of the War Measures Act panicked Laporte's captors into murdering him, that his life might have been spared if the governments had played along with the kidnappers for a while longer. But, of course, this is merely speculation. As to whether circumstances justified the WMA, again one can only speculate. Although the federal and provincial governments implied at the time that there were thousands of armed insurrectionists on the verge of staging an uprising, one of Trudeau's closest associates, Gérard Pelletier, wrote in a book, *The October Crisis*, published in the spring of 1971, that there was no real fear of a popular uprising. Although Pelletier rejected "any notion of a revolutionary rising to overthrow the Quebec government by force," he said there existed the possibility of "grave civil disorders" that justified the invocation of the WMA.[15] Critics have argued that normal police powers were fully adequate for such potential disorders. They note that the group holding Laporte was so weak that they had to take money from their hostage to send out for fried chicken and that Cross, on the day of his release, said, "It was just a case of six kids trying to make a revolution."[16]

It is certainly easier to make a calm assessment of a situation months later than during the tense and chaotic moments when it is developing. But it would be difficult to disagree with the conclusion that the horror of those

October days demonstrated the depth of feeling in Quebec Province. Although few supported the extremism of the kidnappers, there was widespread support for the notion that the French-Canadians of Quebec were not being treated fairly by the rest of the nation. The overwhelming majority that is opposed to violence, even the probable majority opposed to separatism, demand that something be done soon. With unemployment nearly ten percent in the province in the fall of 1971, and the possibility that it might go even higher, the situation becomes more, not less, dangerous. The FLQ is still in existence, although it is impossible for an outsider to know whether its character has changed or its membership is stronger or weaker since the October crisis. No one can predict the course of events in the province. It is certainly clear, however, that the federal and provincial governments are soon going to have to agree on some course of action to reduce the discontent in Quebec Province that is a threat to public safety in the province and to the unity of the nation.

11

Who Owns Canada?

IF THE RELATIONSHIP of English-speaking Canada to French-speaking Canada is the most difficult internal problem, clearly Canada's most difficult external problem is its relations with the United States. A kind of anti-Americanism is growing in Canada. It's not the stone-throwing, library-sacking kind of anti-Americanism that has occurred from time to time in Africa, Asia, and Latin America. Rather it is a kind of gentlemanly anti-Americanism. Anti-Americanism invariably involves students and this does, too, but its most influ-

206

ential practitioners are middle-class, middle-aged, respectable members of the professions and business. Their position is simple. Because of increasing American investment, Canada is in danger of losing its economic sovereignty; if that happens, its political sovereignty is also jeopardized. Most Americans are not aware of this feeling, partly because these anti-Americans (if that is not too strong a term) are not shouters and partly because the United States pays attention to what's happening in Canada only rarely, when extraordinary events like the October 1970 crisis in Quebec demand attention.

If Americans usually ignore Canada, Canadians cannot ignore America. It's just too big and it exerts too much influence on Canada in almost every area of daily life. Foreign trade is vital to Canada, accounting for about one-fifth of its gross national product, and about seventy percent of its exports are sold to the United States. That is not to suggest that Canadian trade is not important to the United States. It is. About one-quarter of American exports go to Canada, which buys about as much from the United States as all of Europe and about twice as much as all of Latin America. But since exports account for less than five percent of the American gross product, only specialists really notice the impact of foreign sales on the American economy.

Because of this enormous dependence upon American purchases, Canada complained bitterly in August 1971 when President Nixon put a surcharge of ten percent on all American imports that were not under quota or other specific arrangements. Although about three-quarters of Canadian exports—such commodities as oil, gas, mineral ores, paper, and newsprint—were exempt from the surcharge, about $3 billion worth of products had to pay it. The exempt products were generally from industries that employ relatively few people, while the products covered by the surcharge came mostly from labor-intensive industries. With Canada already suffering from more than six percent unemployment in the summer of 1971, the surcharge came as a heavy blow. Quebec's premier Robert Bourassa complained that the surcharge could change the unemployment situation in his province from "inadmissible" to "intolerable." As the New York *Times* said on September 5, 1971: "This was to say that in violence-prone French Canada, peace and order, as well as economic well-being might be at stake." A number of American-owned firms also tried to apply the wage freeze to their employees until notified sharply by Canadian authorities that Nixon's order could not apply to Canadian businesses even if owned by Americans.

The surcharge and wage freeze, however, seem likely, as this is written, to be temporary problems, no matter how great. What has concerned many Canadians is the extent to which American investments control Canadian corporations. About half of American foreign investments are in Canada, some $33 billion, returning a revenue of about $2 billion.[1] Such figures are difficult for the layman to comprehend. But the figures that follow are what alarm many Canadians: More than 90% of the factories with more than 5,000 workers are controlled by parent corporations in the United States.[2] Also American-owned are about 99% of oil refining, about 96% of motor vehicles and parts, about 90% of industrial electrical equipment, about 83% of rubber products, about 72% of synthetic textiles, about 59% of industrial chemicals.[3] Speaking in broader terms, Americans own 46% of the manufacturing industry, 58% of the oil and gas industry, and 53% of the mining and smelting industry.

The classic response to concern over foreign investment has been to assert that it is essential to help expand Canada's economy. That was certainly true for decades. The United States sent not only necessary capital but management skills and technology as well.

> No one doubts that American investment has accelerated the pace of economic development in Canada; . . . but it seems also likely to convert Canada into a hinterland of United States industry. . . . To each spurt of expansion there is a corresponding shrinkage in Canada's freedom of action, in its self-reliance, and in its ability to chart its own course for the future.[4]

There are two problems here. One is the need for foreign, primarily American investments, and the long-term effect of those investments. An astonishing fact has emerged about this first problem. According to the November 1970 issue of *The Survey of Current Business*, only about five percent of United States investment in Canada was American money. Most of it came from Canadian earnings and from depreciation and depletion allowances. In other words, *American firms were using mostly Canadian money to buy up Canadian firms.* Nonetheless, few critics advocate a ban on American investment in Canada; they merely want it regulated so that control of Canadian firms does not pass into American hands. This is common all over the world. In fact, no industrial nation in the world has nearly as much of its economy controlled by foreign investors as does Canada. Other nations get worried when foreign ownership approaches ten percent. And this does not mean economic stagnation. Japan, which has severe regulation of foreign investment, has an economic growth rate about four times that of Canada.

It is not the fact of such large-scale American ownership that worries the critics so much as the effects. They are many and influence Canada's economy while diminishing its political sovereignty. One of the ironies is that Canada has sufficient money to invest in its own economy but many, perhaps most, of the subsidiary firms in Canada are wholly owned by American corporations. Despite many requests that Canadians be allowed to buy stock in these Canadian firms, the parent corporations refuse. The reason is obvious. If there were Canadian shareholders, even in a minority position, the subsidiaries would have to justify their policies to them. But these subsidiaries exist for the benefit of the parent corporations in America. They often sell to their parent firms at lower than normal prices and buy from their parents at higher prices. And there are many other financial dealings between parent and subsidiary that would be questioned by Canadian shareholders. Because there are often not sufficient investment opportunities in Canada, Canadians are major investors in the American stock market. Although their investments are generally not enough to gain any measure of control in various American firms, they do provide funds that can be used by these American firms for their own purposes, including foreign investment. Thus, Canadian funds earned by American-owned firms and Canadian money invested in America contribute to the increased American control of the Canadian economy.

There is even more to it than that. Often economic downturns hit Canada and the United States at the same time because the Canadian economy is so influenced by the American. Then Canadian subsidiaries sometimes shut down or curtail their production for foreign markets to protect the jobs of workers in the parent companies. Many Canadians consider this an infringement of Canadian sovereignty. But it goes far beyond that. These American-owned Canadian firms have sometimes refused to do business with countries with whom trade was prohibited by the United States for United States corporations. That meant an area of Canadian foreign policy was dictated by Washington, particularly in trade with Cuba and China. Further, when the United States has balance of trade problems, it issues guidelines to United States firms about the size of its capital investments abroad and the repatriation of foreign profits. The Canadian subsidiaries of United States firms consider that these guidelines apply to them as well. As Herb Gray, Minister of National Revenue, put it:

> The Canadian government thus found itself in the position of having to remind Canadian corporations of the responsibilities of their corporate citizenship. Later, the United States guidelines were made mandatory. We were, in fact, able to negotiate important exemptions for Canada from the U.S. guidelines and these exemptions were highly valued. But the criticism remains that we were in the position—unacceptable, I think, to Canadians generally—of having to negotiate with a foreign government about what would be appropriate practice for Canadian firms located in Canada.[5]

American investments also seriously influence federal-provincial relations in Canada. Although many Canadians, in and out of the federal government, advocate the development of a national policy toward foreign investment, the fact remains that natural resources are the responsibility of the provinces and most provinces resist any national plan that would reduce their power to make their own deals with American investors. If a particular province is having economic difficulty, as most of them are, it is inevitable that it be tempted to make its own deal with an American corporation that might stimulate its own economy. That, of course, is hardly unique to Canada. American states often act in just the same way, offering tax reductions and capital to attract businesses, without thinking of the problems of other states.

> If continental economic integration is in any sense a threat, it is a threat to Canada as a nation. It is not a threat to the provinces as such, many of whom, dependent as they are on American capital and American markets would find it easier to defend their regional interests if they had two senators apiece in the United States Congress than they do at present, when all the pressure on the United States government must be exerted through Ottawa.[6]

Canadian critics of their nation's investment policies also argue that such massive American investment means that Canadian firms do not have adequate research and development programs and do not develop the risk-taking and managerial skills of entrepreneurship, since they are provided by the parent corporation in the United States. They also point out that although Canada has one of the two or three highest standards of living in the world, its economy is very much like those of the under-developed nations in that most of its income comes from the sale of raw or semi-finished materials and most of its purchases are of finished goods. They argue that if Canada did not depend so much on the American economy, it would develop its own essential industries and it would not lose so many of its best people to American firms.

There is no doubt that Canada has the legal ability to change the context of American investment but it is a fearfully complicated matter. Many politicians and businessmen who had been slow to criticize the magnitude of American investment now agree that some sort of regulation is necessary, and a government study has been underway for months. The question is how to regulate it. Many are fearful that a wrong move would mean the loss of investments that might still be necessary. Others are aware that the Canadian economy is almost totally vulnerable to American pressures and they don't want to take any steps that would cause the United States to take reprisals. Then there is the fact that the executives of the American-owned firms have considerable political influence and, needless to say, are lobbying against anything that would hurt their interests.

Although many of them are not, many of these economic nationalists are socialists. They argue that as long as the Canadian economy is capitalist it will not be able to break its dependence on American capitalism. They argue further—especially the members of the New Democratic party—that Canada's social problems, including those of Quebec, can be solved only through socialism. However, most government leaders, including Prime Minister Trudeau, seem convinced that the necessary reforms can be made within the present system.

This economic nationalism has spread to other fields as well. It has increased the concern over the cultural impact of the United States. This is not a new concern. By the end of the 1940s there was growing agreement that a substantial effort must be made to protect Canadian culture from American pressures, powerful, even if largely unintended. A royal commission was named to study the state of the arts. In 1951 Vincent Massey, later to become the first Canadian-born governor general, reported that America's cultural impact was so great that there was a danger it would "stifle rather than stimulate our own creative effort" and he concluded that it was as necessary to spend money for cultural as for military defense; indeed the two cannot be separated." [7] A few years later another royal commission, this one on broadcasting, warned about the threat to "a Canadian identity" from "a tidal wave of American cultural activity." The committee argued that as Canada had used governmental powers "to compensate for our disabilities of geography, sparse population and vast distances" so must it now "apply this system to broadcasting" by spending "quite substantial amounts of money" to strengthen and extend the government-owned Canadian Broadcasting Corporation, since private broadcasters would always depend heavily on American programs. Thus, as we saw earlier, the CBC became the great organ for seeking out and preserving the Canadian identity.

In 1961 still another royal commission studied the status of publications in Canada. It declared that the United States had "the world's most penetrating and effective apparatus for the transmission of ideas" and warned that "Canada, more than any other country, is naked to that force." It pointed out that three out of every four magazines read by Canadians came from the United States and it recommended steps that might improve the capacity of Canadian publications to compete more effectively with larger and richer American publications.[8] These recommendations raised a fuss in the United States, for the commission was talking about *Time* and *Reader's Digest*, two of the most influential magazines in the United States. The commission recommended that money spent for advertising in Canadian issues of foreign magazines be no longer tax-deductible. This would not affect the original United States editions which could enter Canada freely. It meant that special Canadian issues would be less eager to compete for Canadian advertising money. The commission wrote: "It may be claimed that the communications of a nation are as vital to its life as its defenses and should receive at least as great a measure of protection."[9]

President Kennedy himself intervened with Prime Minister Pearson to say that he wanted *Time* exempted from any legislation based on the report of the commission headed by Senator Grattan O'Leary. Pearson had little choice, for Washington suggested that an important trade agreement might not be possible unless Canada exempted *Time*. When the measure was passed by Parliament in 1965, it exempted both *Time* and *Reader's Digest*. Consequently, these magazines are still able to compete in the Canadian market, free of any other American competition.

Time in 1967 had a circulation of 356,000, the most select readership in Canada. With almost all of the editorial product already paid for in the United States, *Time* in 1966 gained $6.5 million in advertising in Canada. One cabinet minister termed the man who puts together the four Canadian pages of *Time* as "just about the most influential newspaperman in Canada." John Diefenbaker, then leader of the opposition, declared in a parliamentary debate that *Time* "has devoted itself to interpreting the news and rewriting it so as to direct Canadian thinking. It has three or four pages of Canadian news in each issue, which makes it a counterfeit magazine when it pretends to be Canadian. It uses these four pages to give its viewpoint, which is not a Canadian viewpoint, to Canadians week after week."[10]

Time and *Reader's Digest* between them in the late sixties took nearly sixty percent of Canadian magazine advertising revenue. This, obviously, made it difficult for genuinely Canadian magazines to survive. The issue is not yet dead, more than a decade after it first came up. Another royal commission recommended in December 1970 "exactly what O'Leary wanted nine years ago: that the exemptions now granted *Time* and *Reader's Digest* . . . be repealed, and the sooner the better."[11]

This 1970 report also said that it was the job of the

Canadian mass media to "help us to define who and what we are."

> We all know the obstacles involved in this task. Geography, language, and perhaps a failure of confidence and imagination have made us into a cultural as well as economic satellite of the United States. And nowhere is this trend more pronounced than in the media. Marquis Childs on the editorial page, Little Orphan Annie back near the classified ads. Nixon and Tiny Tim and Jerry Rubin and Johnny Carson and Lawrence Welk and Timothy Leary on the tube. The Beach Boys and Blind Faith and Simon and Garfunkel on the radio. The latest VC bodycounts courtesy of A.P. and U.P.I. The self-image of an entire generation shaped by Peter Fonda riding a stars-and-stripes motorcycle. Need we continue?
>
> We are not suggesting that these influences are undesirable, nor that they can or should be restricted. The United States happens to be the most important, the most *interesting* country on earth. The vigor and diversity of its popular culture — which is close to becoming a world culture — obsesses, alarms and amuses not just Canadians, but half the people of the world.
>
> What we *are* suggesting is that the Canadian media — especially broadcasting — have an interest in and an obligation to promote our *apartness* from the American reality. For all our similarities, for all our sharing, for all our friendships, we *are* somebody else.

There is criticism of the United States in other areas as well. In November 1970, Jack Davis, who had recently been named by Prime Minister Trudeau to head a new environment department, declared that Canada might hold up the sale of resources badly needed by the

United States. "We're not going to hold up our [natural] gas over Lake Erie—we've just given them enough for five years—but the two problems are interrelated." And he said "the time may come" when the federal government will help Canadians in suing American firms for pollution that spills into Canada.[12] Two days later a colleague, Resources Minister J. J. Greene, discussed the pollution of Lake Erie in similar terms. He said the United States had contributed four times as much as Canada to the pollution of Lake Erie "to the point that Lake Erie may die and the other Great Lakes are threatened, and our ability in our future to further settle and industrialize our shoreline is threatened." Greene also said: "It is to be hoped that the great and powerful nation which can afford to travel to the moon and spend $50 billion a year and more for war will soon be able to afford to clean up its stinking, fouling tons of waste before dumping it into its friendly neighbor's back yard."[13]

Another difference over pollution has developed between Ottawa and Washington. Canada has claimed the waters of the Arctic Archipelago as territorial waters so it can enforce pollution regulations. The United States argues that Canada cannot claim waters beyond twelve miles from its shores, a view held by other maritime states. Canada, however, argues that since those waters may be used in the future by oil tankers, it must be able to establish regulations to prevent pollution. The United States, of course, is one of the nations most likely to use that route if ever it becomes practical. The United States felt so strongly about the matter that President Nixon telephoned Prime Minister Trudeau about it. Thus far Canada has remained adamant.

The range of Canadian grievances is wide. Recently there has been an outcry because American publishers have been buying up Canadian firms, to such an extent that most of what Canadian school children learn about their own nation is from books published by American-owned firms. Even hockey, the Canadian national sport, is dominated by American owners. Of the forty-five commercial hockey teams in North America, all but five are in the United States and all but six are owned by Americans. Also a great many Canadian university graduates have complained that they are unable to get teaching jobs in their own universities and colleges because so many positions are held by American scholars — in some departments of some institutions even a majority. This not only deprives Canadians of jobs that should be theirs, they say, but it means that Canadian students are getting insufficient Canadian content in their courses because the American instructors either do not care about or do not know enough about Canada.

Most of the grievances are directed by Canada against the United States, but one substantial grievance was held by many Americans against Canada: the easy refuge found there by young American men seeking to escape the draft. The very nature of the situation makes exact figures impossible to obtain, but it has been estimated that by the end of 1971 about fifty thousand American youths had fled to Canada, many accompanied by their wives or girl friends. At first Canada provided this refuge somewhat grudgingly, partly because of the long-time identification of the Canadian government with American foreign policy and partly because it recognized that the United States government and many of its citizens would be antagonized by such an action. Yet Canada felt it had no alternative but to recognize the ancient principle of asylum. However, as Canadian opposition to the Vietnam War began to grow, the welcome changed from grudging to open. And from the beginning there were private Canadian groups active in finding homes and jobs for these young Americans, a far from easy task in the recent years of high Canadian unemployment. These Americans have been given the same rights as any other immigrants and can, once they meet the statutory requirements, become Canadian citizens if they choose. It is too soon to know how many will choose citizenship, since five years' residence is required. This may depend to a large extent on whether or not the United States decides in later years to grant amnesty to those who fled the country rather than serve in the armed services during the Vietnam War. In any case, the sense of grievance felt by many Americans has diminished in recent years as opinion in the United States itself has swung against the war.

In the last couple of years, after two decades of following the American lead, Canada has embarked on a more independent foreign policy. In October 1970 Canada recognized the People's Republic of China, a move that started a number of countries toward recognizing China, improved its chances of being seated at the United Nations, as it was in the fall of 1971, and can be said to have led eventually to the agreement between China and the United States that resulted in the invitation of President Nixon to Peking. In May 1971 Prime Minister Trudeau took the trip to the Soviet Union that was postponed by the events of the October crisis. While in Moscow, Trudeau made a point of proclaiming Canada's closeness to the United States as a friend and ally. "But," he added, "Canada has found it increasingly important to diversify its channels of communications because of the overpowering presence of the United States of America. This is reflected in the growing consciousness among Canadians of a danger to our national indentity."[14] The Soviet Union reciprocated in October 1971 by sending Premier Aleksei Kosygin to Canada for a nationwide visit.

The obvious question is: why after all these decades when Canada was an admiring, if sometimes grudging, follower of American leadership has it begun to speak out? One answer might be that Canada is beginning to lose its inferiority complex in relation to the United States. For years Canadians have felt that they had to be educated in an American college, go to plays on Broadway, get their tan in Florida. Artists and writers and performers have felt — as did most of their countrymen — that they hadn't really made it until they were successes in New York or Hollywood. Canadians admired the dynamic Americans, their fantastic economy, their leadership of the "free world." But lately Canadians have begun to lose their envy. Many have been repulsed by the Vietnam War, distressed by the killings at Kent State and Jackson State, concerned about the disintegration of American cities, the spread of drugs, and the increase in crime. In short, America, despite all its admirable qualities, was no longer a country to emulate. Canada should concentrate its energy on being itself, not being a pale America. And inevitably, after all those long years of American leadership, Canada was bound to react, as have other nations that once accepted United States leadership.

So a new Canadian nationalism has arisen and if there is a degree of anti-Americanism in it, it is only because America is right next door with its overwhelming presence. Now Canadians are determined to resist being smothered by that presence and most hope that the United States will understand that they don't mean to be unfriendly, that they only want to protect their identity. A group for just that purpose, The Committee for an Independent Canada, has sprung up and, in a year or two, has established chapters all over the country, although more in English than in French Canada, perhaps because the French identity has never been as vulnerable to the American presence. Its members are not wild-eyed young men but responsible men and women: financiers, university administrators, professors, lawyers, labor leaders, writers, businessmen, politicians, scientists, engineers, broadcasters, journalists, publishers. What they advocate is not a chauvinistic, aggressive nationalism but a constructive, thoughtful affirmation of community. This nationalism is not confined to the membership of organized nationalistic groups. The Gallup Poll, on October 14, 1970, published answers to this question: "Some experts are suggesting that Canada should buy back a majority control, say 51%, of U.S. companies in Canada, even though it might mean a big reduction in our standard of living. Would you approve of this or not?" The replies were 46% in favor and 32% opposed, with 3% giving qualified approval and 19% undecided. If the undecided are divided half and half, that results in a majority of 55% in favor and 42% opposed.

One can hope that such a nationalism could lead to a mutually beneficial relationship with the United States, a better relationship between the federal government and the provinces, and the recognition by English and French that they are all Canadians together and must, for their common good, work out a way to live together in harmony.

Such a nationalism would be good for the United States as well, for it can reduce its old neighbor's grievances only if it understands what they are. Most Americans have a good feeling about Canada and would be distressed to learn that they, even if often unconsciously, have alarmed their fellow North Americans. Beyond that, the inescapable facts of geography and history have decreed that the two nations must live together in intimacy. Each must try to get along with the other. Since the United States has often been too preoccupied with its international concerns to give sufficient attention to Canada, and since it is so much the more powerful, it must be particularly sensitive to Canada's concerns. It can begin by listening.

Acknowledgments

The author and publisher acknowledge, with thanks, permission to quote excerpts from the following books (specific citations of page numbers appear in the Notes, which begin on page 227):

No Mandate But Terror, by George Radwanski and Kendal Windeyer. Grateful acknowledgment is made to the publishers, Simon & Schuster of Canada Limited, for their kind permission to quote from this title.

The Maple Leaf Forever, by Ramsay Cook. We are grateful to the author and to The Macmillan Company of Canada Limited for permission to quote from this book.

The United States and Canada, by Gerald M. Craig. Quotations from this book are reprinted by permission of the publishers, Harvard University Press, Cambridge, Mass. Copyright 1968 by the President and Fellows of Harvard College.

Canada and the Canadians, by George Woodcock. Permission to quote from this book has been granted by the author and the publishers, Oxford University Press, Toronto, and Stackpole Books, Harrisburg, Pa.

Notes

CHAPTER ONE   The Early Years

1   Craig, Gerald M., *The United States and Canada*. Cambridge, Mass., Harvard University Press, 1968, p. 67
2   Discussed by Creighton, Donald, in *Dominion of the North*. Toronto, Macmillan, 1957 (paper), p. 83
3   Discussed by Creighton, p. 97
4   Discussed by Creighton, p. 98
5   Discussed by Creighton, p. 105
6   Discussed by Creighton, p. 130
7   Discussed by Creighton, p. 144

CHAPTER TWO   A Continent Divided

1   Discussed by Creighton, p. 160
2   Cited by Creighton, p. 161
3   Cited by Creighton, p. 162
4   Craig, p. 92
5   Discussed by Creighton, p. 167

CHAPTER THREE   Canada and the New Nation

1   Bemis, Samuel Flagg, *The Latin-American Policy of the United States*. New York, Norton, 1967, pp. 31, 33
2   Morris, Richard, *Encyclopedia of American History*. New York, Harper, 1953, p. 150
3   Woodcock, George, *Canada and the Canadians*. Toronto, Oxford University Press, 1970, p. 298

CHAPTER THREE *(continued)*
4   Woodcock, p. 298
5   Woodcock, p. 299

CHAPTER FOUR   Toward Confederation
1   Discussed by Creighton, p. 244
2   Cited in Creighton, p. 249
3   Craig, p. 129

CHAPTER FIVE   One Dominion—Almost
1   Cited in Creighton, p. 259
2   Cited in Craig, p. 136
3   Discussed in Cook, Ramsay, *The Maple Leaf Forever.* Toronto, Macmillan, 1971 (paper), p. 116
4   Cited in Creighton, p. 310

CHAPTER SIX   The Growth of Canada
1   Cited in Creighton, p. 313
2   Cited in Craig, p. 148
3   Cited in Creighton, p. 374

CHAPTER SEVEN   The New Century
1   Discussed by Creighton, p. 387
2   Creighton, p. 406. A full discussion can be found in Creighton.
3   Discussed by Creighton, p. 409
4   For a discussion of this, see the author's *Beyond Diplomacy*, New York, Parents' Magazine Press, 1970.
5   Cited in Creighton, p. 435
6   Cited in Creighton, p. 435
7   Cited in Craig, p. 176

CHAPTER EIGHT   Full Independence
1   Craig, p. 180
2   Cited in Creighton, p. 441
3   Cited in Creighton, p. 442
4   Cited in Craig, p. 189
5   Discussed by Creighton, p. 456
6   Craig, p. 188
7   Discussed by Creighton, p. 466
8   Craig, p. 200
9   Craig, p. 200

CHAPTER NINE   World War II and After

1   Discussed by Creighton, p. 503
2   Cited in Craig, p. 209
3   Cited in Creighton, p. 512
4   Cited in Creighton, p. 514
5   Cited in Craig, p. 210
6   Cited in Craig, p. 212
7   Cited in Craig, p. 213
8   Craig, p. 218
9   Discussed by Creighton, p. 541
10 Discussed by Creighton, p. 541
11 Cited by Philip Resnick on p. 99 of *Close the 49th Parallel*,
    edited by Ian Lumsden. Toronto, University of Toronto
    Press, 1970 (paper)
12 Department of External Affairs, "Statements and Speeches,"
    April 10, 1951
13 Lumsden, p. 101
14 Cited in Lumsden, p. 102. John J. Deutsch, "Recent American
    Influence in Canada," in *The American Economic Impact
    on Canada*. Durham, N.C., 1959, p. 45
15 Lumsden, p. 104
16 Cited in Lumsden, p. 107, from *Financial Post*, March 25,
    1967
17 The Cuban missile crisis is discussed in full detail, from a
    somewhat unconventional point of view, in the author's *Cold
    War and Counterrevolution: The Foreign Policy of John F.
    Kennedy*. New York, Viking, 1972.
18 Craig, p. 249
19 Craig, p. 252
20 *Toronto Globe and Mail*, January 13, 1963. Cited in Lumsden,
    p. 107.
21 Cited in Craig, p. 254
22 Craig, p. 254
23 Cited in Craig, p. 255
24 Statements and Speeches, March 10, 1967.

CHAPTER TEN   Two Canadas — Or One?

1   Woodcock, p. 163
2   Cited in Woodcock, p. 224
3   Cited in Woodcock, p. 225
4   Woodcock, p. 212

CHAPTER TEN (*continued*)

5   Radwanski, George and Kendal Windeyer, *No Mandate but Terror.* Richmond Hill, Ontario, Simon and Schuster, 1971 (paper), p. 30. The estimate made by the Royal Canadian Mounted Police is probably high, for security services, to be on the safe side, almost always make high estimates in cases like this. I have drawn heavily on the account written by the two Montreal newspapermen, George Radwanski and Kendal Windeyer. The account is sympathetic to the government point of view.

6   Radwanski, p. 32

7   Cook, p. 84

8   Woodcock, p. 234

9   Cited in Radwanski, p. 23

10 Cited in Radwanski, p. 40

11 Cited in Radwanski, p. 41

12 Cited in Radwanski, p. 51

13 Cited in Radwanski, p. 76

14 Cited in Radwanski, p. 81

15 New York *Times*, April 4, 1971

16 Williams, Roger Neville, *The New Republic*, January 30, 1971, pp. 15-18

CHAPTER ELEVEN   Who Owns Canada?

1   From speech by Marcel Cadieux, Canadian Ambassador to the United States, before the Chicago Council for Foreign Relations, April 19, 1971.

2   Newman, Peter C., in *Saturday Review*, March 13, 1971.

3   Facts and Figures on Canadian Independence, Committee for an Independent Canada, Toronto. Undated.

4   Professor Hugh G. Aitken cited in *Silent Surrender* by Kari Levitt. Toronto, Macmillan, 1970 (paper), p. 149

5   Cited in *Canada Today/D'Aujourd'hui*, February, 1971

6   Professor Aitken cited in Levitt, p. 55.

7   Cited in Craig, p. 300

8   Cited in Craig, p. 301

9   Cited in Levitt, p. 8

10 Cited in Levitt, p. 8

11 Cited in *Canada Today/D'Aujourd'hui*, February, 1971

12 Reported in *Toronto Daily Star*, November 19, 1970

13 Reported in *Toronto Globe and Mail*, November 21, 1970

14 Reported in New York *Times*, May 20, 1971

Bibliography

Bemis, Samuel Flagg. *The Latin-American Policy of the United States.* New York, Norton, 1967 (paper).

Canada. The Annual Handbook. Ottawa, Dominion Bureau of Statistics, 1971.

―――― Department of External Affairs. Statements and Speeches, Various years.

Clark, Gerald. *Canada: The Uneasy Neighbor.* New York, David McKay, 1965.

Clarkson, Stephen, Ed. *Visions 2020* Edmonton, Alberta, M. G. Hurtig, 1970 (paper).

Cook, Ramsay. *The Maple Leaf Forever.* Toronto, Macmillan, 1971 (paper)

Craig, Gerald M. *The United States and Canada.* Cambridge, Mass., Harvard University Press, 1968.

Creighton, Donald. *Dominion of the North.* Toronto, Macmillan, 1957 (paper).

Levitt, Kari. *Silent Surrender.* Toronto, Macmillan, 1970 (paper).

Lumsden, Ian, Ed. *Close the 49th Parallel.* Toronto, University of Toronto Press, 1970 (paper).

Morf, Gustave. *Terror in Quebec.* Toronto/Vancouver, Clarke, Irwin, 1970 (paper).

Pope, W. H. *The Elephant and the Mouse.* Toronto/Montreal, McClelland and Stewart, 1971 (paper).

Radwanski, George and Kendal Windeyer. *No Mandate but Terror.* Richmond Hill, Ontario, Simon and Schuster, 1971 (paper).

Simons, James and Robert. *Urban Canada.* Copp Clark, 1969.

Vallières, Pierre. *White Niggers of America.* Translated by Joan Pinkham. Toronto/Montreal, McClelland and Stewart, 1971.

Walton, Richard J. *Beyond Diplomacy.* New York, Parents' Magazine Press, 1970.

Woodcock, George. *Canada and the Canadians.* Toronto, Oxford University Press, 1970; Harrisburg, Pa., Stackpole Books, 1970.

Index